D0710581

*Views*

*of the Irish Peasantry*

*1800-1916*

ERSKINE NICHOL, R.S.A.
from the painting *Home Rule*

# Views
# of the
# Irish Peasantry
## 1800—1916

*edited by*
Daniel J. Casey
and Robert E. Rhodes

ARCHON BOOKS • HAMDEN CONNECTICUT • 1977

©Daniel J. Casey and Robert E. Rhodes 1977
first published 1977 as an Archon Book,
an imprint of The Shoe String Press Inc.
Hamden, Connecticut 06514

Printed in the United States of America

*Library of Congress Cataloging in Publication Data*

Main entry under title:

Views of the Irish peasantry, 1800-1916.

    Bibliography: p.
    Includes index.
    1. Peasantry—Ireland—History—Addresses,
essays, lectures. 2. Peasants in literature—
Addresses, essays, lectures. 3. English litera-
ture—Irish authors—History and criticism—
Addresses, essays, lectures. I. Casey, Daniel J.,
1937-    II. Rhodes, Robert E., 1927-
HD625.V53    301.44'43'09415    76-39913
ISBN 0-208-01630-9

To the memory of Martin J. Waters,
Associate Professor of History at the Cooper Union
in New York City,
who died at age thirty-five in Dublin,
in April, 1974,
and to the memory of Kenneth H. Connell,
longtime Professor of Economic and Social History
at the Queen's University of Belfast,
who died in Belfast in 1974.

*Their contributions to the study of Irish
peasant life have greatly enriched interdisciplinary
Irish studies.*

# Contents

# Preface

In Seamus O'Kelly's novel *Wet Clay* the young American whose Irish parents have sent him "home" to Galway to work the land discusses the future with his grandmother. She tells him that, with all his learning, he should have been a priest. He answers that he has no religious vocation, that he has followed his blood and become a peasant.

Such a response might have spilled the tea on the tablecloth, if indeed there had been a tablecloth. Instead, there is a shock of disbelief.

"'A what?' the old woman asked."

"'A peasant—we're all peasants, are we not?'"

"'Faith, I never knew that until you came across the ocean to tell us,' the old woman said."

For the Irish the word "peasant" carries an awesome historical approbrium, evokes dreadful images in the folk memory, and rankles the imagination. As Estyn Evans explains it, "We readily apply the word to cultivators of many parts of Eurasia but hesitate to use it for our own rural people." But a collection of essays that attempts to describe the conditions of the Irish people in the 1800-1916 period, in realistic rather than romantic terms, can hardly ignore the word. No synonym—not "countryman" nor "folk" nor "rustic"—will do as well.

In this collection the editors have consciously resisted an arbitrary definition of "peasantry." We cannot or will not bind the contributors to an *OED*-like definition that offers "one who lives in the country and works the land" or one that

9

somehow conjures up the vision of an English retiree cultivating his rose garden. In a multidisciplinary collection such as this, "peasant" necessarily takes on a wide spectrum of meanings depending upon the background of the writer and the discipline. Martin Waters, an American historian, identifies peasant Gaelic Leaguers by references to occupation, education, language, birthplace, and mobility; Alf MacLochlainn, an Irish librarian, refers to the peasantry as a "rural proletariat."

Perhaps Patrick Kavanagh, who created Maguire in "The Great Hunger" and who understood the people of the cottages because he was one of them, provides the consensus. "Although the literal idea of the peasant is of a farm working person," he says, "in fact a peasant is all that mass of mankind which lives below a certain level of consciousness. They live in the dark cave of the unconscious and they scream when they see the light." Scholars will, of course, modify the poet's definition, but they will hardly quarrel with that notion that it is the psychological restraint imposed on the peasant that damns him to eternal darkness, that destroys his positive self-image and erodes his confidence in the culture that has made him what he is. Then, it is not a reticence to come to terms, so much as a need to broaden the understanding of "peasant" for humanists that cautions against denotation. The editors believe that the fuller and more satisfactory definition of "peasant" will emerge from the totality of the essays contained in the collection.

The Irish, having weathered centuries of British occupation and endured the rigors of penal laws meant to effect genocide, averted cultural annihilation by their determination to survive and to survive as Irishmen. Despite the successes of the foreign plantations and the rash of short-lived rebellions, the native Irish entered the nineteenth century with language and customs virtually intact.

But the Act of Union (1800) dissolved the Dublin Parliament, vesting Westminster with full control, and brought with it shocking colonial mindlessness. The Irish peasantry, left to an uncertain future, now faced a century and more of political dependence on an absentee government in London. Throughout the 1800s famine, famine-related diseases, and emigration came to be the accepted lot of the landless poor. After a period of decline that was alarming rather than gradual, the language of the country was by mid-century spoken by less than a quarter of the population and written by only a fragment of those native speakers. There was a general dissolution that struck at the roots of the culture; and there was the inevitable loss of *duchas na nGael*, the Gaelic heritage.

The ancient civilization that absorbed Norsemen and Normans and outlived centuries of British domination and survived the flight of the Gaelic nobility finally stood on the threshold of extinction. The nineteenth century began with the murmur of a "de Profundis" that seemed to signal the end of a distinct Irish society. That requiem proved to be premature, however. There was a language still spoken in isolated Gaeltacht pockets and a persistent culture in less affluent, rural areas of the country. The indomitable Irishry had cast their minds on bygone days and preserved remnants of a tradition that stubbornly refused to die.

The irony of nineteenth-century Ireland is that it is perhaps best remembered in the public mind for a literary revival sponsored by Yeats and Company. The very name "revival" implied a kind of cultural quietus and conjured up visions of bare ruined choirs, windswept castles, and pre-Celtic megaliths. But the Poet recognized that romantic Ireland had passed, that he had only shreds of folklore and mythology gathered from the peasantry, together with the writings of a dwindling and romanticized Anglo-Irish gentry with which to fashion a movement. The Celtic Renaissance never actually attempted resurrection; it shifted about in the shadow of the past and built a new literary tradition in English on the dim vestiges of the old. The old culture defied translation. Apart, then, from the aura of the romance—the images of the cheerful, rag-clad peasants that

graced the pages of Lover, Lever, and Hall—there were also
the harsh realities of nineteenth-century Irish life to be
reckoned with and there was the despair out of which grew
a nationalism that would not be silenced. There was, too, the
sense of urgency for preserving something of the shrunken
legacy. *Views of the Irish Peasantry, 1800-1916*, deals with
the realities, the despair, and the need for cultural survival.

The essays that follow are by recognized American and
Irish scholars. A number offer exciting, original theses; some
extend existing research; a few challenge the classic con-
cepts about the period. Taken together they provide an
informed commentary on the social, political, and economic
issues and contribute to a fuller understanding of the peasantry and of an important era in Irish history. Alf Mac-
Lochlainn emphasizes that it is from the nineteenth-century
peasantry, "that great lumpen-proletariat," rather than from
the chieftains and the great castles, that the modern Irish
derive their heritage and that the failure to distinguish
between the non-Gaelic tradition of the Big House and
Gaelic peasant legacy has contributed to the existing confusion about the Irish past.

In his survey of peasant beliefs of the period, Estyn
Evans begins with an understanding that a peasant is, after
all, a person tied to a particular place and that his customs
and beliefs are forged, to a great degree, by the natural
environment of that place. He examines fascinating *piseoga*
(folk beliefs) that have carried into nineteenth- and twentieth-century Irish life from antiquity, *piseoga* that have
become cultural imperatives for the native Irish today. Ned
Lebow's study of British images of poverty in pre-Famine
Ireland, on the other hand, analyzes the ways in which the
non-Irish viewed the Irish peasantry. More importantly, it
underscores some of the ways in which the British have
rationalized their attitudes toward the Irish and ways in
which those attitudes have contributed to the further impoverishment of native Irish traditions.

The rebellious Irish peasant altered the personality of

his greatest folk hero—made him both hero and anti-hero. As part of the larger view of Finn MacCool in the folk tradition of the nineteenth century, James MacKillop suggests that the Irish peasant turned to guile and cunning to deal with law and landlord. His hero, to remain a hero, would have to follow suit. And D. K. Wilgus claims that if we added the narrative songs to the remainder of the folksong tradition, the reflection of nineteenth-century Ireland would be more complete than the picture of any people in any other period. The research by Wilgus, a preface to his cataloguing of Anglo-Irish narrative folksong, offers excellent insights into the rich musical tradition and into the minds of the people whose songs they were. Maurice Harmon finds his primary focus in William Carleton's stories of the Irish peasantry and in the social history and lore that Carleton has preserved in his tales. Professor Harmon adds to the critical reassessment of the most significant peasant writer of the pre-Famine period and provides, as it were, standards against which other and later portrayers of the peasantry can be measured.

Martin Waters, in "Peasants and Emigrants: Considerations of the Gaelic League as a Social Movement," is forced by subject and discipline to define "peasant" in more objective terms. Not only does he objectify with respect to origin, education, occupation, native language, and mobility, he sets out the premise that, more than has been heretofore credited in research, it was the peasantry who were responsible for developing a strong national consciousness through the offices of the Gaelic League.

In a consideration of the influence of peasant backgrounds on the life of W. B. Yeats, John Unterecker finds that the poet's intimacy with the peasantry contributed more than has been supposed to his view of Ireland. William Butler Yeats's reflections on his Sligo boyhood are, of course, scattered through the works, from *The Celtic Twilight* to "Under Ben Bulben." Here Unterecker examines the poet's relationship to the people and traces a theme that has up to now been sublimated in the criticism. Jack B. Yeats, the well-known painter and brother of W. B. Yeats, also had fond recollections of his Sligo years. Many of those recollections impinge on his artistic consciousness. Marilyn Gaddis Rose treats Jack Yeats's rendering of peasant types in an essay that analyzes artistic techniques and establishes the artist's attitude toward the folk he sketched and painted. And John Messenger's bibliography is rich enough to indicate the wealth that awaits those who would pursue the elusive Irish peasant of the nineteenth and early twentieth centuries beyond these readings.

The young American in *Wet Clay* can no more be faulted for exalting peasant past or peasant blood than his grandmother can be deprecated for her incredulity. Somewhere between the aura of youthful romance and the spectre of experienced reality there is, after all, a multifaceted truth that touches the gnarled and twisted roots of nineteenth-century Irish life. In *Views of the Irish Peasantry, 1800-1916*, the editors have attempted to reproduce just that sort of truth and establish a unique, period composite of the peasant in Ireland.

This collection contains original essays on the Irish peasant of the late nineteenth and early twentieth centuries, essays in anthropology, art, economics, folklore, history, literature, musicology, political science, and sociology. It grew out of a "Conversations-in-the-Disciplines" Grant awarded the editors by State University of New York Research Foundation to sponsor a triduum on the theme in April, 1973. The papers have undergone a good deal of additional research in the months that have passed. It is safe to say that the Irish peasant has never before been subjected to scholarly scrutiny from so many disciplines in a single volume.

State University of New York

DANIEL J. CASEY
ROBERT E. RHODES

*Views*

*of the Irish Peasantry*

*1800-1916*

ALF MACLOCHLAINN

# Gael and Peasant— A Case of Mistaken Identity?

IT IS NOT DIFFICULT for Americans considering events in Northern Ireland to recognize that the events in the post-1969 period had their origin in a movement exactly patterned on an American model. Even the acronymic title of the Northern Ireland Civil Rights Association betrays an American influence, and the politics of street demonstration in defense of minority rights, in alliance with student activism, make clear that the model was in fact the black movement in the United States.

Americans are, however, unaware that there is another civil rights movement organized and articulated in Ireland, a movement for the defense of the rights of people living in the Irish-speaking areas of the country. The restoration of the Irish language as the general vernacular, or at least one general vernacular of the country at large, has been a declared aim of all governments of the Twenty-Six Counties from the foundation of the state until this year. It has shared a place of honor among national objectives with the restoration of national unity. But with the failure of Southern Irish governments to achieve national unity or equal rights in the North for the nationalist minority, the struggle for civil

Alf MacLochlainn is Director of the National Library of Ireland in Dublin. He has written widely in Irish and English, mainly on aspects of cultural history.

rights was taken onto the streets. And failure to make
progress in the restoration and extension of the Irish language has led those most concerned, the people of the Irish-
speaking districts, to organize their own civil rights campaign.

A spokesman for the Irish-language civil-rightsmen, recently asked what the objective of the movement was, said,
*"Na taoisigh agus na caisleáin mhóra."* "The chieftains, and
the great castles." The chieftains and the great castles of the
Gaelic order, it should be pointed out, disappeared from the
land over three hundred years ago. The spokesman's alle-
giance to them and his hope that they be reinstated epito-
mized an elaborate and deceitful model on which much of
modern Irish politics is based, and this paper will emphasize
a pervasive confusion between the Gaelic civilization, remote though much publicized, and the nineteenth-century
peasant culture, recent but ignored.

The above model proposes that Ireland was a saintly,
happy, pastoral, and aristocratic society until the English
invaded in the twelfth century. For a few centuries she
successfully absorbed the invaders until, with the Reforma-
tion, they became Protestants and land-grabbers. Cromwell's massacres and the following expropriation of land
and persecution of the Catholics almost destroyed the old
civilization. Almost but not quite. It lived on in the homes of
the ordinary people who made sporadic, futile attempts to
overthrow their oppressors now and again. At last, in the late
nineteenth century, a group of leaders, political, cultural,
and revolutionary, came upon the scene at the same time
and set in motion a process which culminated in the re-
establishment of Irish independence.

By rights, one might have thought, the chieftains and
the great castles of old would have been reestablished
overnight. They were not, of course, and we are entitled to
ask wherein is the model faulty? It is faulty in one glaring

respect, from the point of view of the modern historian: it
fails to qualify.

One of the nationalist movement's most active, articulate, and persuasive proponents was Alice Stopford Green,
the widow of John Richard Green, author of a notable short
history of the English people. Mrs. Green was associated
with the writing of the history, a solid, liberal and optimistic
view of the development of Britain. But only after J. R.
Green's death did she develop an interest in Irish history.
Her major work in the field, *The Making of Ireland and Its
Undoing*,[1] a much-needed defense of Ireland's earlier institutions, stood against the ignorance and biases so notable
in the work of earlier English historians. She extolled the
mercantile achievements of late medieval and early modern
Ireland and analyzed the Gaelic system, but at no point did
she make any suggestion about the size of the population of
Ireland. The changing population level was, however, a
vital factor in the history of the Irish cultural community that
we are considering.

How then has our model been propagated and why was
it so beguiling? The answers to these questions may be
found in the social and intellectual history of Ireland in the
nineteenth century. The social historian's visit to the nineteenth-century Ireland is a nightmare. In the early part of the
century he finds a teeming rural proletariat increasing
rapidly in numbers, exerting continually increasing pressure
on limited food-producing resources, living in abject squalor and degradation and chronic famine. By the middle of
the century a population of eight millions (it had doubled in
fifty years) was totally dependent on the potato for sustenance and when that failed, the population dwindled as
rapidly as it had risen.

Think of just one measure and illustration of the squalor
of the living conditions and the obliteration of the population. Our rural proletarians—they have never called them-

selves peasants or peasantry and have always felt those
words to be terms of condescension—our rural proletarians
of, let us say, 1825, lived in mud cabins. A family of six or
more persons and their animals, perhaps a pig and a cow,
were the occupants. The poorest slept on straw on the dirt
floor and one visitor describes an early morning call which
revealed to him the father of a family sleeping with his hair
matted in the excrement of the cow.[2] In the intercensal
period 1841-1851, the time of the greatest famine, 360,000 of
these cabins, the homes of two million people, completely
disappeared.

In the second half of the century the prospect is equally
depressing. We see now an emerging petty bourgeois class,
the usurious shopkeepers who had survived, the small-town
merchants, the lower professionals in a better-organized
British administration, a client class living like the rest of the
United Kingdom on the exploited riches of the booming
British Empire.

A survey of the press of the late nineteenth century
reveals that Ireland was, for this class, a cultural desert. The
theater was a bad third to English provincial touring theater,
and poetry was a second-rate imitation of English types.
Religion, for the majority, was in the hands of a church
which had barely held its own in control of the huge earlier
population and could now, as it were, relax and impose its
will. Its will was a high level of unquestioning religious
practice in ever bigger and uglier churches in monumental
and classical styles that were the norm until comparatively
recent times. For the Protestant minority, religion was low-
church, rather dour and definitely anti-papist, and legally or
not, it was establishment.

Education of a kind was available. A national system of
elementary schools had been set up in the 1830s. The Christian Brothers and other congregations of religious, as well as
providing many of the elementary schools, were providing

secondary education for the sons and daughters of the middle class. A Royal Commission on Education in 1876 reminds us that the Christian Brothers publish their own school books which are "much more difficult than the National series—and fuller of interesting matter of all kinds, and combine nationality and Catholicity in considerable proportions."[3]

A friendly witness tells us something more of the Christian Brothers schools:

> The success of the pupils in after life is proverbial. As tradesmen, shop assistants, junior clerks and other employees, the boys educated in the Christian schools are eagerly sought for. Some of them have risen to high positions. Not many years since, one of them who by his ability and integrity had honorably won for himself a high commercial status, filled the office of Lord Mayor of Dublin.[4]

Even these shop assistants, tradesmen, and junior clerks included some sensitive souls who felt keenly the cultural deprivation of living in a provincial back-water off the mainstream of British life. Some opted for that mainstream and left for London, but such expatriations were naturally the exception.

Those who remained behind also did something about it. The Gaelic Athletic Association was founded in 1884, devoted to the regulation and extension of the national brand of football and to other athletic sports. The Gaelic League was founded in 1893, committed to the preservation and extension of the Irish language. Literary and politico-literary societies of earnest young men led ultimately to the formation, on the one hand, of Sinn Fein, a political organization seeking economic independence and, on the other, of the whole modern literary movement—Yeats, the Abbey

Theatre, and all that followed. The Irish Socialist Republican Party was founded in 1896. There were, too, what we would call the little magazines, advocating various advanced positions on national issues.

All of these things were supported, the Gaelic Athletic Association and the Gaelic League in particular, for the reason that once you educate people to be tradesmen, shop assistants, and junior clerks, they want something more. As the old Union song said, "We want bread and roses, too." Though they were now literate and above the starvation line, they were part of a wealthy empire and yet cut off from what we call the establishment. There was no un'versity for them; the learned professions were for the wealthy who could afford the training and the well-connected who could profit by it.

There was a vice-regal court in Dublin where the Lord Lieutenant went through all the motions of levee, drawing room, and presentation, but again only the wealthy and the well-connected would reach the invitation lists. So few of these were Catholics that a particular term of derision or approbrium had come into use: they were Catholics, but Castle Catholics, from their admission to Dublin Castle where the vice-regal court was held. The shop assistants and junior clerks needed some rationale for the urge to self-expression, and the intellectuals who had remained free of the British connection provided it. In fact they adumbrated the opening phases of the historical model I have already outlined. "We Irish," they said, "are descended from ancient kings." If one writes his name in the Irish language on his milk-cart or over his shop, he is manifesting a nobility above and beyond anything that the jumped-up descendants of the Cromwellians or these Castle Catholics can boast of.

Douglas Hyde was a founder of the Gaelic League. His essay on the de-Anglicization of Ireland was one of the foundations documents on the new movement. For an indifferent, second-rate imitation British culture, he wanted to substitute something "racy of the soil."[5] The phrase has a faintly Nazi ring about it, though Hyde was a most gentle and humane person. In 1893 William Larminie published a collection of Irish folk-tales with an introduction that is a totally racist exposition complete with Aryans.[6] These men were reasonably free of overt racial prejudice, but they lived in the age of the theory of evolution; their expositions were a defence of something they treasured rather than an attack; they were actively combatting the even more racist British attitude which placed the Irishman and the Negro at the bottom of a human scale which began just above the ape.

Arthur Griffith, founder of Sinn Fein, was nearer than Hyde to being the junior clerk—Hyde was a son of the rectory—and Griffith saw an Ireland controlling its own destiny, not necessarily entirely separated from Britain, but as a rejuvenation of the Ireland Mrs. Green was to describe. The view is that so savagely lampooned by Joyce in a famous passage in which the Citizen describes Ireland's trade with Europe and her cultural eminence in the headlong vernacular English spoken by ordinary Irishmen:

> Where are our missing twenty millions of Irish should be here today instead of four, our lost tribes? And our potteries and textiles, the finest in the whole world! And our wool that was sold in Rome in the time of Juvenal and our flax and our damask from the looms of Antrim and our Limerick lace, our tanneries and our white flint glass down there by Ballybough and our Huguenot poplin that we have since Jacquard de Lyon and our woven silk and our Foxford tweeds and ivory raised point from the Carmelite convent in New Ross, nothing like it in the whole wide world! Where are the Greek merchants that came through the pillars of Hercules, with gold and Tyrian purple to sell in Wexford at the fair of Carmen?[7]

Hyde had learned Irish from the peasants of Roscommon, a boggy and desolate county west of the Shannon. Yeats had walked with Lady Gregory as she collected folktales from the peasants of Clare and Galway. Patrick Pearse, younger than the others and destined to be the sacrificed Messiah of the movement, came to his extreme nationalist position by work for the Gaelic League and by living among the Irish-speaking peasants of Galway.

To return now to the model, simply expressed as "all Gaels are descended from kings and the objective of the nationalist movement is to restore the glories of ancient Erin," one might suggest that what Hyde, Yeats and Pearse experienced in the West had little to do with Gaelic supremacy or the glories of ancient Erin. They were, in fact, meeting the remains of the recent and vigorous culture which had flowered in the population boom of the early nineteenth century.

In 1891, a census year, the western seaboard counties of Ireland contained half a million Irish speakers, and, on average, one third of the population of each of these counties spoke Irish; as high as forty-eight percent and fifty percent in Galway and Mayo. I refer repeatedly to these western counties, not only because they were and are the main repository of the Irish language as a vernacular, but for another reason, a demographic and I think a significant one. It was in these counties that the catastrophic population drop in the years following the Famine was at its most dramatic. We have already noted the disappearance of the miserable dwellings of two million people. In Ulster, eighty-one percent of those houses disappeared (Ulster includes the western seaboard county of Donegal), in Connaught seventy-four percent, in Munster sixty-nine percent and in Leinster, with no Atlantic littloral, sixty-two percent, least of all. As to the population decrease in the intercensal period 1841-51, Leinster lost only fifteen percent, Ulster only sixteen percent—that is, the population outside Donegal remained stable—Connaught lost twenty-nine percent, Munster twenty-four percent.

It must be remembered that there were more Irish-speaking people in the country in the 1840 period than ever before or since, and the areas where Irish was most spoken were those which experienced the most extreme rise and fall in population. To go into the reasons for this might serve to distract the reader from the premise that any Irishman who is descended from a king is so descended via the teeming lumpen-proletariat of rural Ireland of the early nineteenth century, and that any such *ultimate* descent is about as relevant to twentieth-century movements and their objectives as his descent from Adam, or as O'Casey had it, "the skeleton of the man of Java." And one might hold, analogically, that the shared, though remote, African ancestry of American blacks is less relevant to twentieth-century matters than their shared and much more proximate experience of servitude and deprivation in North America.

Why did Yeats and Pearse and the rank and file—Hyde was less guilty—adopt the aristocratic model we have been outlining? It seems that it was a case of being men of their time. The pervasive imperialist air they breathed was filled with the smell of powder and blood from the far-flung outposts of the Empire. The hero of the popular magazines was the dashing young subaltern on the Northwest Frontier of India dying for queen and country under a hail of Jezail bullets. Why does Pearse constantly use the word "splendid"? Of course they rejected the notion of British racial superiority, but instead of proposing the genuine alternative—that there is no racial superiority—they posited an Irish racial superiority. Listen to Pearse on O'Donovan Rossa, a dead Fenian:

And here we have the secret of Rossa's magic, of

Rossa's power: he came out of the Gaelic tradition. He was of the Gael; he thought in a Gaelic way; he spoke in Gaelic accents. He was the spiritual and intellectual descendant of Colm Cille and of Seán an Díomais. . . . To him the Gael and the Gaelic ways were splendid and holy, worthy of all homage and all service; for the English he had a hatred that was tinctured with contempt. He looked upon them as an inferior race, morally and intellectually. . . . [8]

Both Yeats and Pearse adopted the figure of the youthful hero Cuchulainn for their particular ideological and literary purposes. Cuchulainn was was the hero of the tenth-century saga, a great champion at arms, a great lover, one who stood absolutely alone in defense of his country when all her fighting-men were stricken with weakness. Important to note is that Cuchulainn was known to latter-day readers only through the work of scholars on ancient texts. He figures hardly at all in the folktales of the peasantry and then only as a debased trickster lacking the epic proportions of the saga.

The leaders were men of their time in that they were products of the intellectual history which preceded them as well as of the atmosphere which surrounded them. That history for a hundred years or so, for a period, that is, spanning the rise and fall of our rural population, starts with the Romantic movement. More specifically it begins with MacPherson's *Ossian,* the great literary hoax of the eighteenth century. On the slimmest basis in genuine folklore, the Scots poet MacPherson produced verse in English celebrating the legendary hero Ossian. (I should perhaps point out that until relatively recent times Ireland and Scotland formed a single linguistic community; the Gaelic of Scotland is a dialect of the Irish language.) Ossian, the Celtic hero in the mist of Scottish bogs, was God's gift to the Romantics. In a painting from the age, Napoleon's marshalls arrive in paradise to be welcomed by Ossian. The name Oscar, from one of the figures in the Ossianic cycle, also became popular in literary circles and is widely dispersed at present.

In 1789 Bishop Percy produced his *Reliques of Ancient English Poetry*, and in 1791 Miss Charlotte Brooke in Ireland produced her *Reliques of Irish Poetry*. It was a self-conscious expression of nationalist sentiment, and it is not surprising that she should have been moved to act in competition, as it were, with Percy. Miss Brooke's class—she is of the family of Viscount Brookeborough, sometime Prime Minister of Northern Ireland—was enjoying a period of self-assertion in an Irish parliament which, although woefully limited in its powers and in its representative character—there were no Catholics in it—had regained some independence from Westminster. Here is Miss Brooke:

> The productions of our Irish bards exhibit a glow of cultivated genius,—a spirit of elevated heroism,—sentiments of pure honour,—instances of disinterested patriotism,—and manners of a degree of refinement, totally astonishing, at a period when the rest of Europe was nearly sunk in barbarism: And is not all this very honourable to our countrymen? Will they not be benefited,—will they not be gratified, at the lustre reflected on them by ancestors so very different from what modern prejudice has been studious to represent them?[9]

And the Romantic element for her treatment is clear from her use elsewhere in her preface of "plaintiff tenderness," "tender pensiveness," and "epic majesty" as terms to describe the quality of the verse she is presenting.

The independence of the Irish parliament, such as it was, was short-lived, and it was absorbed into the United

Kingdom by the Act of Union in 1800, but the expression of
Romantic literary nationalism continued into the early nineteenth century with a short-lived society for the preservation
of the Irish language, and especially with the poet Thomas
Moore. His verse is largely unread today, though some of his
songs survive deservedly in performance and contain a lyric
statement of what was to become the conventional model.

> Rich and rare were the gems she wore,
> And a bright gold ring on her wand she bore;
> But oh! her beauty was far beyond
> Her sparkling gems, or snow-white wand.
>
> "Lady! dost thou not fear to stray,
> "So lone and lovely, through this bleak way?
> "Are Erin's sons so good or so cold,
> "As not to be tempted by woman or gold?"
>
> "Sir Knight! I feel not the least alarm,
> "No son of Erin will offer me harm:—
> "For though they love women and golden store,
> "Sir Knight! they love honour and virtue more!"

And again:

> Let Erin remember the days of old,
>     Ere her faithless sons betray'd her;
> When Malachi wore the collar of gold,
>     Which he won from her proud invader;
> When her kings, with standard of green unfurl'd
>     Led the Red-Branch Knights to danger;
> Ere the emerald gem of the western world
>     Was set in the crown of a stranger.[10]

"Moore's Melodies," as they were called, became and have

remained almost to our own day the respectable middle-class expression of Irish nationalism.

As we move into the middle of the century, we meet the Young Ireland Movement, the local manifestation of Young Europe, and perhaps, therefore, the last expression of the Romantic movement. Its ideologue was Thomas Davis, a young Protestant intellectual who was, before Pearse, the most articulate exponent of a particular form of nationalism. Davis died tragically young in 1845, after only three years of the existence of the Young Ireland newspaper, *The Nation*, and it is in his essays for that paper that we find his political views. He was a fine writer, intelligent, well-informed, broad-minded, serene, and entirely free of racial or religious prejudice.[11] His attitude to the culture of the mass of the people was humane and indulgent, but avowedly elitist. He had a great respect for verse, music, and song as vehicles of propaganda, and he envied the Germans and the Scots their great national collections. He took it upon himself, however, to prescribe what Irish verse should be about and urged writers to supply specific wants. For the existing popular verse he had little respect. Davis said:

> The Irish-speaking people have songs by the thousand, but they (especially the political ones) are too despairing; the poor, who are limited, (and therefore, in some sort barbarised) to English alone, have only the coarsest ballads, where in an occasional thought of frolic, or wrath, or misery, is utterly unable to redeem the mass of threadbare jests, ribaldry, mock sentiment from the heathen mythology, low thoughts, and barbarous misuse of the metres and rhymes of the language. The middle classes are forced to put up with snatches from those above and below them, and have less music than either.
>
> We want the verse-writers of Ireland to try and

remedy all these wants. If they be poets, they can do so.[12]

And of the music, he says that it is the greatest achievement of the Irish people, telling the history, the climate, and the character, "But it too much loves to weep.... Music is the first faculty of the Irish. And scarcely anything has such power for good over them. The use of this faculty and this power, publicly and constantly, to keep up their spirits, refine their tastes, warm their courage, increase their union and renew their zeal—is the duty of every patriot."[13] His own verse, unfortunately, was hardly good enough to fulfill these noble or socialist-realist objectives.

By a sad irony, Davis and his colleagues contributed something—how much cannot be quantified—to the decay of the Irish language which they so enthusiastically befriended. *The Nation* newspaper was entirely in English and was a country-wide success, reaching a circulation of ten thousand, ahead of all rivals. Davis himself had recommended an Irish-language newspaper as a safeguard for the language, but his verse and the verse of his colleagues in *The Nation*, extolling the virtues of the Gael, was all in English. It was the work of these poets and of Moore which was to be at the root of the nationality which we have seen linked with Catholicity in the Christian Brothers' readers.

Another strand in the intellectual history was the uneasy contact between the liberal intelligentsia and the masses. There had been a violent popular uprising in 1798, allied with an attempt at French republican and revolutionary intervention. There was a minor military attempt in 1848, a rising organized by the Young Ireland movement. It was defeated and the leadership again sought alliance with European radicalism. Again in 1867 there was a rising by Fenians hoping for American arms and for aid from Civil War veterans. Militarily that, too, was a failure, but it fed the iconography of both Yeats and Pearse.

These intellectual movements somehow ignore the eight million peasants and their real, vivid, and concrete way of life. They had a culture, an intense and distinctive vernacular culture, a culture expressed in music, song and dance, social amusements, shared superstition, marriage and funeral customs, housing styles, seasonal observances, organization of craft work, all the things we now call folklife, and all things which owed nothing at all to the chieftains of the Gaelic order who were dead and gone two hundred years and more. Their culture existed as a function of their being there, eight million of them spread over the land in their hundreds of thousands of cabins, a self-contained community of pre-industrial proletarians in a vast rural congested slum.

People sharing such a culture acquired a tolerant, kindly, easy-going attitude to life, an attitude spiced with witty conversation; they became, in fact, urbane country-dwellers. And it is this urbanity which so beguiled Hyde, Pearse, and indeed all but the most insensitive who, since then, have lived in or even visited the Irish-speaking districts. That this culture survived best in those districts was a result of historical and demographic determination, a coincidence and not a condition. Of course their culture had no means of expression comprehensible to the Establishment, no press, no academies. It reached the level of those who had the press and the academies only by accidental and devious routes.

Traditional music is a case in point. The music of the Irish harp was moribund by 1800. But the Romantic antiquarianism of the Miss Brooke type had generated an interest in the dying art, and in 1794 a number of gentlemen—note "gentlemen"—in Belfast organized a harp festival. A number of harpists, all elderly, were brought to the city and an outstanding pioneer musicologist, Edward Bunting, transcribed their music. Now this music, like much European folkmusic, is modal in character, that is to say, it is not built on the major and minor keys which were the Establishment convention. In other words, the drawing rooms would have found the native Irish tunes exotic and difficult. Accordingly a composer named Stevenson took the tunes and arranged them in the conventional scales as the melodies for Thomas Moore's lyrics. In this "bowdlerized" form they gained currency as Ireland's national music. Happily, all the harpists were dead by this time and were spared the experience of hearing them.

Most contemporary documentation on the vernacular culture came from the comments of visiting travelers or of would-be reformers. They had no spokesman of their own. None, except perhaps William Carleton, a novelist and short story writer of outstanding qualities, who, in a sense, had turned his back on them. He was a peasant in origin and was able to be a spokesman for his people only, as we say, by taking soup; that is to say, by giving up the traditional Catholic faith of his family and becoming a Protestant. So, like Moore's melodies, Carleton's stories were inaccessible to the people from whose lives they drew their ultimate inspiration. They were published mainly in the *Dublin University Magazine*, a sophisticated conservative organ which was certainly not read in the remote villages.

Of course there were people who knew what was happening. The catastrophic effect of the Famine was well-known; but not so well-known was the cultural eclipse which was accompanying it. Sir William Wilde, father of Oscar Wilde and husband of one of the poets of *The Nation*, was both a demographer and a cultural historian. He was a doctor and the official commentator on the death-tables which accompanied the census reports. He was also a contributor to the *Dublin University Magazine* and there he wrote: .

The old forms and customs, too, are becoming

obliterated; the festivals are unobserved, and the rustic festivities neglected or forgotten; the bowlings, the cakes and the prinkums (the peasants' balls and routs), do not often take place when starvation and pestilence stalk over a country, many parts of which appear as if a destroying army had but recently passed through it. The hare has made its form on the hearth, and the lapwing wheels over the ruined cabin. The faction-fights, the hurlings, and the mains of cocks that used to be fought at Shrovetide and Easter, with such other innocent amusements, are past and gone these twenty years, and the mummers and May-boys left off when we were a gossoon no bigger than a pitcher. It was only, however, within those three years that the *waits* ceased to go their rounds upon the cold frosty mornings in our native village at Christmas; and although the "wran boys" still gather a few half-pence on St. Stephen's Day, we understand there wasn't a candle blessed in the chapel, nor a *breedogue* seen in the barony where Kilmucafauden stands, last Candlemas Day; no, nor even a cock killed in every fifth house, in honour of St. Martin; and you'd step over the *brosnach* of a bonfire that the childer lighted last St. John's Eve.[14]

And if that passage requires extensive glosses to be fully comprehensible, it merely shows how different from ours was the culture described.

To resume the American analogy, one might suggest that all the leaders and spokesmen we have mentioned so far are, if the peasant be the black, either whiteys or Uncle Toms—sympathetic, humane whites, benign Uncle Toms—but always at a remove. One spokesman who escapes this criticism deserves special mention—James Fintan Lalor, the agrarian radical. He was no landless laborer, but he was of a country farming family and not of the urban middle-class intellectual elite, and he saw with intense clarity what was really happening. He, like Davis, was to die before the dreadful decade of famine had run its course and he wrote: "For those same land-owners are now treading out the very life and existence of an entire people, and trampling down the liberties and hopes of this island for ever. It is a mere question between a people and a class—a people of eight million and a class of eight thousand. They or we must quit this island . . . they or we are doomed."[15] Note that he speaks in the first person. "They or we are doomed," whereas Davis, despite all his qualities, speaks to his reader as if the Irish peasant were a third party. Within half a century of Lalor's death, the bulk of what remained of the Irish peasantry had become landowners and *we* were doomed.

At the end of the century a combination of Romantic nationalism, second-hand racialism, European radicalism, middle-class frustration, and cultural awareness, generated the literary revival, the Gaelic League, Sinn Fein, and 1916. To a degree the independence movement was successful. It produced an independent Irish state, though not one consisting of the whole island. Its constitutions used Irish names for the houses of the legislature, for the great public offices. Now the prime minister is *Taoiseach*, the very word for "chief" which the Irish-language leader from Connemara used in the interview quoted earlier.

But if the name of the prime minister is a Gaelic word, his office and function are entirely British. We have a ceremonial head of state, a bicameral legislature, a ministry which is appointed by and holds office at the pleasure of the elected legislature. The schools—primary, secondary, and university—are as founded by the British. Our money, weights, and measures, are British. Our mainstream culture, like Britain's, is fast becoming mid-Atlantic. The eight million proletarians who were the real progenitors of the cul-

ture which enchanted Hyde, Yeats, and Pearse, are completely forgotten.

A state brought to birth with these strange parents—
misguided antiquarianism and the forms of modern parliamentary democracy—is bound to have personality problems. It was basically xenophobic. Irish writers who published abroad were purveyors of foreign filth. Censorship
flourished and was welcomed. John McCormack, a tenor
who was made a Papal count and sang Moore's Irish melodies, was a national hero. Literature and song had to con-
form to the old standard; they had to affirm that the maiden
could walk from one end of the island to the other and no
man would steal her jewels or her maidenhead.

But now that there was an independent democratic
state, who needed to write his name in Irish on his cart to
affirm his nobility? Was it not sufficient guarantee of quality
to be a senator or a member of a national commission? When
the risen peasant took his big house in a fashionable Dublin
suburb he called it by a Gaelic name and the atavistic pieties
were fulfilled.

There is really no escape from the Procrustean model to
which our parents and grandparents have shackled the Irish.
They are republicans, yes. Everybody in 1977 knows that
monarchy is a music-hall joke. They are separatists, yes, if
that is what is shown by wanting to go mid-Atlantic or
European with Irish institutions nominally guiding us, and
not as a third-rate British apanage. But Gaels? The chieftains
and great castles are as remote from real life as the trappings
of the monarchy. The Irish-speaking areas shrink continu-
ously, if at varying rates, and as the Irish language dies, a
vociferous crowd gathers for the wake; but as demographic,
political, and other forces, native and foreign, destroy the
distinctive proletarian culture of rural Ireland, hardly anybody seems to know or care.

[1]Alice Stopford Green, *The Making of Ireland and Its Undoing, 1200-1600* (London: Macmillan, 1908).

[2]James Connery; *The reformer, or an infallible remedy to prevent pauperism and periodical returns of famine, with other salutary measures for the support of the destitute poor, for the enforcement of cleanliness, suppression of usury and establishing the futility of the plan of William Smith O'Brien . . . to mitigate any of those grievances in Ireland. Also, several amendments . . .*, 5th ed. (Limerick: pr. by G. and J. Goggin, 1833), p. 44.

[3]*Report of the Commissioners appointed to enquire into the nature and extent of the instruction afforded by the several institutions in Ireland for . . . primary education.* 1870. Vol. II, p. 156.

[4]John Nicholas Murphy, *Terra Incognita or the Convents of the United Kingdom* (London: Longmans, 1873) p. 515.

[5]Douglas Hyde, "The Necessity for De-Anglicising Ireland." In *The Revival of Irish Literature.* Addresses by Sir Charles Gavan Duffy, Dr. George Sigerson and Dr. Douglas Hyde (London: T. Fisher Unwin, 1894).

[6]William Larminie, *West Irish Folk-Tales and Romances* . . . (London: Elliot Stock, 1893).

[7]James Joyce, *Ulysses* (London: The Bodley Head, 1947), pp. 310-11.

[8]Patrick Pearse, "O'Donovan Rossa: A Character Study." In *Collected Works of Padraic H. Pearse: Political Writings and Speeches* (Dublin: Phoenix Publication, 1924), p. 128.

[9]Charlotte Brooke, *Reliques of Irish Poetry* (Dublin: pr. by George Bonham, 1789), p. vii.

[10]Thomas Moore, *A Selection of Irish Melodies with . . . Characteristic Words by Thomas Moore*, Vol. I, nos. 1-2 (London: Power, 1808), pp. 40, 84.

[11]I have since investigated Davis's racialism more closely and must sorrowfully withdraw my acquittal. (*Irish Times,* Nov. 20, 1973).

[12]Davis's essay on the songs of Ireland as reprinted from *The Nation* by M. J. Barry as introduction to his *Songs of Ireland* (Dublin: Duffy, 1845), though not in later pious editions of Davis's works.

[13]As quoted in *The Poems of Thomas Davis (now first collected with notes and historical illustrations)*, ed. T. W. (Dublin: Duffy, 1846), p. 36.

[14]Sir William Wilde, "Irish Popular Superstitions." In *Dublin University Magazine*, 33, May 1849, p. 544.

[15]James Fintan Lalor, *Collected Writings, with a Biographical Note by L. Fogarty.* Revised edition (Dublin, Talbot Press, 1947), pp. 62-63.

E. ESTYN EVANS

# Peasant Beliefs in Nineteenth-Century Ireland

THERE ARE CERTAIN deep-seated attitudes and beliefs which come close to being universal among the world's peasantries but which take on local color and strength from long association with a particular environment. Such environmental relationships have been neglected by students of peasant life and peasant attitudes who see their subjects in the light of their own special interests—whether as cooperating villagers or kinship groups; as producers of wealth or as the victims of landlordism; as natural poets or base villeins; as patriotic rebels or pious supporters of one of the universal religions—without much regard for regional variations. Yet, in essence and by definition, a peasant is a person tied to a particular place—to the *pays* from which the French word *paysan* is derived. And it is the tenacity with which he clings to the soil, and the soil clings to him, that gives a peasantry its endurance and its character. The peasant is not normally a political animal, but he can be roused when his rights in the land are threatened. To interpret peasant culture we need, therefore, to examine and analyze in each region the cultural landscapes which the peasantries of the world have fash-

E. Estyn Evans is Emeritus Professor of Geography and Chairman of the Institute of Irish Studies at Queens University in Belfast. Professor Evans has written nine volumes and over two hundred scholarly articles on human geography, archaeology, and folklore. His latest book-length publication is *The Personality of Ireland*.

ioned, in forms that are intimately related to environmental opportunities, and to the accumulated experience of life in particular environments. And in this essay, we should consider the peasants of the nineteenth century in the light of a long inheritance.

If we look at the Irish countryside and the Irish countrymen of the nineteenth century with this idea in mind, I think we might hesitate to refer to Ireland as a peasant country in the full sense of the word. It is true that in the late eighteenth and during the first half of the nineteenth century, before the Great Famine, when cereals were in demand for export and when an almost exclusive dependence on a single food-crop, the New World potato, made arable husbandry of a kind an essential element in Irish country life, the word "peasant" would seem applicable. But for the greater part of Irish history, before the adoption of this alien food crop, the pastoral habits proper to this damp evergreen habitat predominated and set their stamp on the landscape and on the people. At the worst, stockmen can move with their flocks and herds and are not tied to the soil, whereas the peasant, whether in Ireland or Egypt or China, holds on, whatever befalls. In the west of Ireland to this day a farmer measures his land not by the acre but by the "cow's grass"; that is, by its grazing capacity: "I have the grass of ten cows." And although it could be said that peasant attitudes to the land , which were later fostered by the campaign for peasant proprietorship, came in time to characterize Ireland, there remained, and still remains, a strong pastoral flavor about Irish rural society. The countryman would rather have cow dung than soil on his hands, and the care of livestock is his preferred occupation. His walk and his roving eye are those of the stockman rather than of the man who drives a plough and keeps his eye on the furrow. Not only do livestock and livestock products still make the single largest contribution to the country's wealth, but old food habits persist, for the

Irish consumption of milk and milk products is *per capita* the highest in the world. The Irish landscape, even to the tops of the hills, is bitten bare by centuries of grazing activity, and the once universal forest cover of this well-watered island had been greatly reduced so long ago as the Neolithic Age, in the fourth and third millennia B.C. Most of the "virgin forests" of the age of the Virgin Queen were of dubious virtue.

Kinship ties appropriate to animal breeders have tended to be stronger than ties of place or bonds of context: the word "friend" was commonly applied until recently only to a person to whom one is related by blood. Another aspect of this adjustment between life and landscape is the nature of rural settlement. We note the virtual absence of what is an almost universal concomitant of peasantry, the nucleated agricultural village, which in the ancient agrarian landscape of the Old World has typically attracted a population of hundreds and frequently of thousands. Concentrations of this order of magnitude in Ireland are not villages but towns, or at least settlements having urban functions. A recent official report on the Donegal Gaeltacht makes reference to "the large town" of Falcarragh: it has a population of 366! The old Gaelic order rested to a great extent on wealth in cattle, and its epic literature is loud with the bellowing of bulls. It had little use for towns, large or small. Seasonal gatherings at hallowed sites sufficed for the needs—commercial, political, and social—of scattered communities who came together for short periods at the turning points of the year, notably at the beginning of summer, May first, when the springing grass beckoned herds to the hills, and the beginning of winter, November first, when harvests and livestock were all gathered about the homestead. As we shall see, many customs and beliefs persisting in nineteenth-century Ireland have to do with these critical dates: indeed, because dues paid in cattle were collected at these times of

stock taking, they are still the days when rents are due—even
if they are not always paid. (This applies nowadays only to
urban property, farm holdings being almost entirely owner-
occupied under Land Purchase schemes.)

In contrast to the village community, the preferred
settlement of the Irish countryman is the lone steading, the
isolated holding. It is a cultural feature of deep significance.
The rural ascendancy, whether in Gaelic or Anglo-Irish
times, had always lived in this fashion, in family units, as had
the freemen of "strong farmers." The peasant, too, though
he clung to small kin-settlements or "clachans" into the first
half of the nineteenth century in many parts of the country[1]
increasingly adopted the isolated dwelling and holding as
his prospects improved in the years after the Great Famine.
The care of livestock was facilitated by the close association
of the family with its animals, especially with milk cows and
calves which need constant attention; and the relationship
was often very close, with practical as well as magical
purpose.

The byre-dwelling, as it may be called—a small-scale
variant of the west European long-house in which, however,
there was no division between the human and the animal
ends of the house—persisted well into the last century in
much of the west and northwest of the country. It is recorded
of County Tyrone early in the century that "one house
answers for the family and the cow for more than one third
of the peasantry,"[2] and further west in County Donegal, as
late as 1841, nearly half the houses had one room only,
though many were the homes of landless laborers who had
no cows. Even at the end of the century the Reports of the
Congested Districts Board reveal that in the remote parts of
County Mayo cattle were kept in most of the houses. There
must have been grave problems in maintaining tolerable
standards of hygiene under these conditions, but hygienic
considerations, at any rate, were overridden by the desire to

conserve under cover as much dung as possible for the spring crops. Moreover, it was considered "lucky" to have the cows living with the family, and the warmth engendered in a low-roofed room, measuring perhaps no more than 12 by 20 feet, at most 15 by 30 feet, was mutually beneficial. It should be borne in mind, however, that in other parts of the country different conditions prevailed; for example, in most areas in eastern Ireland even the humblest tenants had been accustomed, possibly since Anglo-Norman times, to live in houses designed solely for human habitation. Dwellings of this ancestry, probably deriving from the "hall and bower" house of medieval England, have the chimney in a central wall dividing the house into two rooms.

In writing about nineteenth-century rural Ireland, then, we should be careful to distinguish among different regions and among different layers of the population. Equally we should keep in mind the differences, in economy, demography, political and tenurial conditions—and particularly, so far as our present topic is concerned, in devotional practices of the Catholic population—between the first and second halves of the period, roughly before and after the Great Famine. In place of the popular notion of a pious peasantry eagerly demonstrating its devotion to the faith under penal or near penal conditions, during the first half of the century it was precisely in the more rural areas, where the clergy was in general less well-educated and had to serve rapidly growing populations, that laxity, vice, and violence were most prevalent, and, it may be presumed, reliance on the elder faiths most widespread.[3] The devotional revolution of 1850-1875, associated particularly with Archbishop Cullen, made the great mass of the Irish people practicing Catholics,[4] but this is not to say that the elder faiths were vanquished. I recall a piece of advice given a few years ago in the Sperrin Mountains of County Tyrone to a veteran collector working for the Irish Folklore Commission, Michael J.

Murphy: "Leave old thorns and priests alone," he was told, "give them their dues and leave them alone." This could be the text for a discussion of traditional beliefs in much of nineteenth-century rural Ireland. The spread of Victorian notions of propriety and respectability which helped to weaken the grip of the elder faiths in the course of the century was no doubt facilitated by improved methods of communication and by the steady advance, in the second half of the century, of that eminently Victorian innovation, the railway, and its travelling companion, the clock. But again I can quote the remark of a practitioner of traditional cures in County Cavan made not long ago: "Some people waste time quacking around with doctors before coming to me for the cure."[5]

In areas where tradition was strong there was a sense of kinship with the natural world and at the same time a sense of the supernatural. The human family should set nature a good example, and an annual birth was the expected contribution of a wife to general well-being. Infertility in a woman was a much-dreaded blemish, not only because it deprived the family of helping hands but also because the fertility of herds and crops was sympathetically affected by human increase. Sickness of any kind was not only a misfortune but a disgrace, a sign that luck had forsaken one and evil forces were working against one. The supernatural world was always present.

Ailing children were often hidden from prying eyes, though if they survived, however maimed, they found a place in the community in roles such as music-making, which did not demand the physical strength of work in the fields. The medical fact that male children are more vulnerable than females was interpreted as the result of malice, for males were preferred and cherished, if only because a male was "another spade in the bog." If a thriving child, perhaps weaning, became a whining brat he was regarded as a changeling; the envious fairies had stolen the child and placed one of their ailing members in its place. There is still, in many parts of Ireland, a tradition that a child should not be praised but be addressed in abusive terms, as a "rogue" or a "tory," for if the fairies should overhear children being praised they might become envious and either bring them ill-luck or steal them. Well into the present century, for I myself have come across it—in County Cavan—boys into their teens were dressed in petticoats and long frocks in order, or so it was believed, to mislead the thieving fairies. These were particularly active and malicious on May Day and at Halloween.

Sympathetic magic as defined by anthropologists seems to offer the best explanation of many of the tenacious beliefs and practices of rural Ireland. For many years I have studied archaeological and ethnographic evidence for the early diffusion and secular persistence of a cultural pattern which had its origins in pre-Celtic antiquity and which proved capable of absorbing and assimilating new elements brought in by successive intrusions, whether Celtic warriors, Christian missionaries, or Anglo-Norman knights. I see as a symbol of this continuity the great stone monuments and burial cairns which in their hundreds have dominated the cultivated landscapes and hill pastures through three, four, or five millennia. They testify to the faith of their builders in the mysterious powers of nature, and on the whole their survival in the midst of the fields and the pastures which they fashioned has justified that faith, though there are marginal areas in the north and west of the island where an over-exploited environment has retaliated by burying prehistoric fields and monuments in extensive peat bogs. Celtic legend interpreted the Great Stone Graves of pre-Celtic Ireland as the bridal beds of Dermot and Grania, built by the eloping couple for their nightly comfort as they fled across the country. In this explanation we may see a reflection of the primary purpose of these monuments as instruments of fertility. And well into the last century it was believed, in parts of the country, that the best hope of success for a childless couple, when all other means of procuring a child had failed, was to spend a night on one of Dermot and Grania's Beds. The close association of birth and death, an association which is also evident in many of the customs connected with wakes for the dead as recorded in recent centuries,[6] may perhaps be explained by the assumed presence in such places or at such times of ancestoral spirits, possibly in the form of fairies, waiting to be reborn. That Irish Christianity inherited some of its magic from the elder faiths is suggested by the transference from a Giant's Bed to a Saint's Bed of powers of conveying fertility. Countless holy wells resorted to for cures similarly owe their virtue to an older magic. A strong whiff of the supernatural hangs around them. No less than a hundred such wells have been counted even in the metropolitan county of Dublin—some of them still visited at appropriate seasons—although they were regarded by the Dublin establishment as "the height of popish superstition."[7]

While the early church, conditioned to the agrarian practices of the Mediterranean world, had encouraged the cultivation of cereals and vegetables, it had to come to terms with the pastoral world when it reached the Atlantic edge of Europe, and it appears scarcely to have touched, despite its wooing and winning of the milkmaid Bridget, a hidden world of antique practices and beliefs relating to livestock and particularly the milk cows. Many of these persisted into the nineteenth and into the first half of the twentieth century. The luck of the herd was linked with certain flowering bushes, especially the whitethorn and the rowan, whose bounteous white May blossoms brought the promise of a full flow of milk through the summer, and with yellow flowers such as the marsh marigold which carried the promise of butter in their golden cups. Well into the last century the May Boys in the west of Ireland would sing as they paraded on May Day, the first day of Summer (in Lady Wilde's translation):

> Summer! Summer! the milk of the heifers
> And ourselves brought the Summer with us,
> The yellow Summer, and the white daisy,
> And ourselves brought the Summer with us.[8]

The veneration accorded to whitethorn bushes—fairy thorns—certainly outlived the nineteenth century and is by no means forgotten; and that the power of the lone thorn still rivals that of the priest in the mind of some countrymen is suggested by the advice given to a folklore collector as quoted above. The thorn tree is a wise native that does not normally flower until the danger of killing frosts is over, and I suggest that its first magic blossoming is at the sun-lit edge of Neolithic clearings in the dark forest.[9] If I am right, this is an illustration of what Frazer called the laws of Similarity and Contagion, principles by which magic forces are invoked for procuring health, luck, and fertility.

Similarly, it was for magical rather than practical reasons that many plants and herbs were utilized in the numerous folk cures that were practiced into the last century and have survived in some areas to this day. Some of the cures no doubt depended on genuine medicinal properties discovered pragmatically, and some recipes were probably borrowed from the common stock of a European pharmacopoeia, but who can say that the medicinal virtue of the foxglove first resided not in *digitalis* but in the gift of the unseen forces whose "fairy fingers" fitted the spotted flowers (folks' gloves)? More obviously, sympathetic magic was invoked as a cure through color association. Thus yellow flowers such as buttercups were pressed into service as a cure for jaundice, but in most cures nature was wisely given an alternative chance of displaying its healing powers by the injunction that the patient must rest for a fixed number of days. I quote a recipe which illustrates the treatment of illness. "Drink three times at a well to which you have been led on a bridle by a person whose parents had the same surname before marriage." One further example to illustrate the principle of "like for like" will suffice. The lesser celandine, one of several "golden harbingers" of spring, bears the popular name of pilewort (root). When the poet Wordsworth wrote "There is a flower the lesser celandine that shrinks . . . ," it is doubtful, despite his familiarity with the folklore of the Lake District, whether he deliberately used this word in its full significance, but the name pilewort derives from the virtue of the plant as a pileshrinker. The reason is not far to seek. The root of the celandine is a cluster of fleshy lobes which quickly wither when the plant is pulled out of the ground.

It was believed that for every illness an appropriate cure had been provided in the plant world, though not everyone had the secret knowledge and the correct formula to make use of it. The latter in their precision seem to have occupied the place of the chemical formulae of scientific medicine. Newcomers to the Irish flora—and there are many—have not gathered about them the same wealth of folk beliefs, but it may be said that around every native plant, tree, shrub, bird, insect, and animal there had grown through centuries of observation, experience, association, and the play of the human imagination, an immense body of legendary lore to which Seán O Súilleabháin's *Handbook* is a monumental guide.[10] Occasionally one can see a logical argument in favor of traditional cures that seem at first sight to be both irrational and unhygienic. Thus the use of animal dung in the treatment of burns—or in the plaster applied to chimney canopies—can be understood in the light of its capacity to resist the passage of air or smoke. The real virtue of cow's urine taken as a medicine to treat a great number of ailments depended perhaps on its sterility, but the explanation of its power is revealed in the euphemism, "all flowers' water," for it was believed to contain the healing essence of all the herbs the cows had eaten when grazing.

It seems also that sympathetic magic could work merely by sight. There is a delightful story told in that charming book of reminiscences of "The Tailor," which is full of insights into the peasant mind in one of the most truly Irish districts in all Ireland, West Cork. A farmer had a prolific bull whose fame was such that envious farmers who were less fortunate would walk for miles to see it; and the owner found it profitable to charge the sightseers for the privilege. On one occasion a poor farmer came to see the bull, but explained that because he had such a large family he could not afford to pay the full price, though he would give all he had in his pocket for a look at the animal. The owner asked him how many children he had, and when he was told there were seventeen he replied: "Keep your money and stay where you are: I'm going to fetch the bull to take a good look at you."[11]

The power of these magic forces was greatest, as we have seen, at the turning points of the pastoral year and on cosmic occasions such as mid-winter and mid-summer, when the sun itself "turned" in the heavens. The period between mid-summer and the beginning of "harvest" (autumn) on August first was a critical time. In earlier centuries whitemeats (milk products) were available for the summer herders, but in general July was "the hungry month"—and in Ulster, at least, the time for fighting—for there were many years when the previous year's harvest had been exhausted before the beginning of August. On St. John's Eve (June 23) the continued vigor of the mid-summer sun, now about to decline, was encouraged by communal dancing and by a

blaze of "bonefires." St. John's Eve was also a favorite time
for visits to holy wells, which were often appropriately
dedicated to the water saint, John the Baptist. In the rites
practiced at holy wells, carefully guarded stones shaped like
limbs and other parts of the ailing body played a part in
cures, and cup-marks gouged in stones—or, in their Christian counterparts, scored crosses—also figured in the healing processes.

Above all, the four quarter-days (February 1, *Lá Fhéile
Brighde;* May 1, *Lá Bealtaine;* August 1, *Lá Lúnasa;* and
November 1, *Lá Samhna*)[12] were held in high esteem. They
might be compared to four hinges in a protective screen
wrapped around the peasant world. Supernatural powers
could most easily gain entrance to the world of nature at
these break-points in the round of the year, particularly at
the beginning and end of the summer half-year, May first
and November first. The power of the fairies, for good or ill,
was strongest at the beginning of May. If this was the most
dangerous time of year to be stricken with illness or ill-luck,
it was also the time when the appropriate cure or remedy
was most effective. It was believed that the fairies were
particularly active in Maytime because , as at Halloween
also, they were changing their dwellings, a belief that probably reflects folk memories of the ancestral custom of
"booleying," the seasonal movement of summer pastures
which was maintained in the west of the country well into
last century. Although the common grazing grounds were
referred to as "mountain," they were not always located in
the high hills, for there were many other stretches of un-
enclosed land of poor quality where flocks and herds could
obtain adequate nourishment only on free range and therefore required to be herded. The long leisure of summer days
was conducive to music making, story telling, and the
practice of simple handicrafts, and it was under such conditions that the Gaelic language and oral traditions lasted

longest. The Irish countryman's remarkable powers of speech, whether in Gaelic or Anglo-Irish, probably owes something to long familarity with an oral tradition, including much legendary history, that was memorable precisely because in a pre-literate society it was made to be remembered. That much of this highly imaginative lore, when fossilised in print, has passed for historical fact has had tragic consequences in post-Famine political ideology, particularly when combined with the gift of eloquent oratory and with the tendency to violence which seems also to go with societies deeply concerned with kine and kin. Looking back to the formative stages of Gaelic adjustment to the Irish environment, it seems likely that the territorial bases of the many petty kingdoms were defined in relation to the availability of summer pastures. Wars between rival chieftains frequently took the form of cattle raids.

Some of these ancient kingdoms have preserved their titles in popular speech down to the present day, e.g., the Kingdom of Mourne,[13] and in general an intense loyalty to historic territories persisted through the first half of the nineteenth century and delayed the emergence of national patriotism among the rural population. It is ironic that "the idea of an Irish nation, rooted in history" was the romantic discovery of the burghers of Belfast at the end of the eighteenth century.[14] And while we may not agree with Arnold Toynbee's assertion that "the Irish are a byword for their prolonged failure to create an effective united Irish state,"[15] or at least would not express it in this way, it cannot be denied that territorial and political fragmentation and inter-regional or inter-group rivalries, which for the last half century have been most conspicuously displayed in Ulster, have been common features of Irish life since pre-Norman times.[16] One recalls inter-monastic feuds, the tithes claimed by abbots on the loot of cattle raids, and the burning of churches, which, popularly regarded as a prerogative of the

Norsemen, in fact began before Viking times and is still in evidence.[17]

A favorite pastime of the giants of Irish legends was hurling boulders at each other, and that this was a projection of a prevailing custom is suggested by the persistent habit of stone throwing, whether as a game among country school children or with more serious purpose in the streets of Belfast and other towns. Giraldus Cambrensis wrote in 1185: "The Irish are quicker and more expert than any other people in flinging, when everything else fails, stones as missiles, and such stones do great damage to the enemy in an engagement."[18] Here again we may see pastoral habits at work, for before the adoption of the herding dog in the sixteenth century, flocks and herds were controlled by casting or slinging stones at straying animals. In this environment stones are never far to seek, and they took the place of the clods of earth which were the missiles of shepherds in the softer regions of Europe. I think one may attribute some other traits of the Irish character, also, to what I have called the pastoral tradition: a certain lack of tidiness and of concern for appearances, a weak sense of visual art and craftsmanship, an indifference to aesthetics, comfort, and privacy, and a general "throughotherness." It is of interest to observe that this word is applied to, and may find its origin in, the chaotic arrangement of small arable strips in the infields attached to rundale clachans, and could equally refer to the formless disorder of the clachans themselves. Tidiness on the other hand is a virtue, if virtue it be, associated with the wheat farmer and the villages of the English tradition.

But I must return to the cycle of the year and say something more of the other great festivals which have marked its course until recent times. It seems that the summer months, defined by the May and November festivals, were so well recognized as the period when young folk left home that when seasonal migration in search of work took them from the west of Ireland to the richer east and to Britain, the accepted dates for leaving and returning were May 1 and November 1.[19] The winter half year, on the other hand, was the time for other enterprises; above all it was the marriage season. Down to the period of the Great Famine, between eighty and ninety percent of all rural weddings took place in the winter months, and the marriage season reached its climax at Shraft-Shrove Tuesday.[20] To get married in May was regarded as particularly unlucky, possibly because a first child could then be expected in the lean days of late winter but also, perhaps, because this was the time of year when the families were regarded as being at greatest risk.

The demographic history of nineteenth-century Ireland has had many interpretations, but most students agree that in this as in so many other matters the Famine was a great divide. It seems that only after the Famine was the now familiar pattern of late marriage (and non-marriage) established, although it had already been very general in western Europe for about a century. Here again, therefore, the Famine marks the end of beliefs and customs—in this case early and universal marriage—which might be described as prehistoric. This apparent aversion to marriage among the peasantry, which has been attributed mainly to economic forces such as land legislation,[21] led to no less than a quarter of their number never marrying. Yet illegitimacy rates were low, and one may well ask what compensatory outlets were found. "Drink and dogs, horses and gambling, religion, even the bombing and burning of Border posts have been seen as the Irishman's way out."[22] Emigration was another way out. Judging by the content of sexual obscenity in the anonymous threats which one has seen as part of the appalling violence displayed in Northern Ireland during recent years,

I would be inclined to agree that sexual repression has been one of the factors involved. Increasingly, too, as the nineteenth century advanced and gave way to the twentieth, as fairs and patterns declined and with them the faction fighting which had been a traditional outlet for violence, fighting between groups of different religions, Protestant and Catholic, became a frequent occurrence. (Stick fighting, with the defensive hard hat as a consequence, comes naturally to cattle-drovers, and like stone-throwing should be seen as a pastoral *damnosa hereditas*.) It was in Ulster, where the customary tenant right gave the peasant a sense of part-ownership, and in County Armagh, where holdings were exceptionally small, that competition for farms led to sectarian violence and the formation of the Orange Order in 1795.

The mid-point of the summer half-year was celebrated in the festival of *Lúghnasa*, originally on August first. It was a half-way festival also in another sense, for while *Bealtaine* remained frankly pagan and *Samhna* was largely won over by the festival of All Saints, *Lúghnasa* was characterized by a mixture of pagan and Christian rites. This applied also to the corresponding mid-winter festival of St. Brigid, held on February first. *Lúghnasa* was also a time for fairs often known as Lammas or gooseberry fairs. It was formerly, perhaps, the time when visits were made by those left in charge of the winter homestead to the young folk tending the flocks and herds in the hills or by some lake in the bogs. *Lúghnasa* rites are especially associated with hill tops and with water, but while many places were visited merely for berry picking and picnicking, some of them had long been taken over by the Catholic Church and turned into pilgrimage sites. Thousands of pious pilgrims still make the arduous ascent of the Reek (Croagh Patrick in County Mayo) on the Sunday before the first day of August. It is

Ireland's holiest mountain, and its pilgrimage is made on the most celebrated Sunday of the year. Many Patrician legends have gathered around it since the seventh century, but other traditions clearly have pagan associations. The fact that its popularity waned in the second half of the nineteenth century—before its artificial revival in the present century—suggests that the driving force in its secular popularity had been commemoration of a seasonal festival.

It was a first-fruits festival, marked by the gathering of bilberries and by many ritual performances which have been carefully collected and analyzed by Maire MacNeill,[23] who counted over a hundred such hilltop assemblies in nineteenth-century Ireland, and listed nearly a hundred local names, in Irish and English, applied to the day of the festival, e.g., Harvest Sunday, Garland Sunday, Height Sunday, Bilberry Sunday. Its fame rested partly on the guarantee of plenty as fruits began to ripen and harvests turn to gold towards the end of "the hungry month," when the previous year's harvest had been exhausted. It could well be that other processional gatherings such as the notorious Orange Marches which, taking place in "the hungry months," had led to periodic outbursts of violence, have origins that are older that Orangeism. They, too, have their associated bonfires.

Finally, at the end of summer, came Halloween. For the rural population it was, like the first day of summer, a time when the other world was omnipresent. The spirits of the dead walked and visited their old earthly homes, and the fairies were much given to stealing young women. This was another occasion for lighting bonfires, as it had been in other parts of the British Isles before the Guy Fawkes anniversary (on November 5) stole its fire. All appropriate seasonal tasks must be completed before the first of November, and superstition spurred on the indolent. All unpicked fruit, for example, was said to be fouled by a supernatural being at Halloween. Another example of the function of superstition—in this case to serve a wise ecological purpose—was the springtime advice given to children, that if they stole the eggs of wild birds their fingers would be blistered. Many Halloween games now played by children were once acts of prognostication, involving fruits such as nuts and apples which had been gathered in. But I need not elaborate on the theme that, through much of the nineteenth century, peasant life was closely geared to the rhythm of the natural environment and the related cycle of work and that the care of cattle was a central element in the cycle.

In this essay I have tried to set the Irish peasant of the nineteenth century, anthropologically and enthnologically, against his environment. I see the crisis of the middle of the nineteenth century as marking in many ways the end of prehistory. At the same time the tensions produced by the fundamental changes in rural society brought about by the Famine appear to have resulted in secret recourse to supernatural forces during the second half of the century and, in some parts of the country, well into the present century. I believe that an approach to the understanding of peasant life in nineteenth-century Ireland through historical and literary records misses two important dimensions in so far as it does not tap the hidden sources of oral tradition and use the evidence of the cultural landscape as a clue to the nature of the folk who made it. In his sense of oneness with the living past and in his intimate relations with the forces of nature, the Irish peasant or the Irish countryman, during the first half of the century, at any rate, was pagan rather than Christian. But increasingly he came to seek the propitiation of spiritual powers by prayers under the banner of orthodox religion. By and large, All Saints had taken over the composite virtue of All Flowers.

[1]E. E. Evans, *The Personality of Ireland* (Cambridge: University Press, 1973), p. 60. At the first Census in 1821, only six percent of the Irish population lived in towns of more than 2000 inhabitants; in 1841, when half the population of Britain was urban, the proportion was still only fourteen percent.

[2]J. McEvoy, *Statistical Survey of the county of Tyrone* (Dublin: The Dublin Society, 1802), p. 69.

[3]I borrow the term from a remarkable pioneer work, W. G. Wood-Martin, *Traces of the Elder Faiths of Ireland*, 2 vols. (London: Longmans, Green & Co., 1802).

[4]Emmet Larkin, "The Devotional Revolution in Ireland, 1850-1875," *The American Historical Review*, 77 (1972), pp. 625-652.

[5]Beatrice Maloney, "Traditional Herbal Cures in County Cavan," *Ulster Folklife*, 18 (1972), pp. 66-67, 79.

[6]S. Ó Súilleabháin, *Irish Wake Amusements* (Cork: Mercier Press, 1967).

[7]Caoimhin O Danachair, "Holy Well Legends in Ireland," *Saga och Sed*, Uppsala, 1960, pp. 35-43.

[8]Lady Wilde, "Irish Popular Superstitions," *The Dublin University Magazine*, 33 (1849), pp. 541-60.

[9]E. E. Evans, *Irish Folk Ways* (London: Routledge and Kegan Paul, 1957), p. 272.

[10]S. Ó Súilleabháin, *A Handbook of Irish Folklore* (Dublin: Educational Company of Ireland, 1942.)

[11]Eric Cross, *The Tailor and Ansty* (Cork: Mercier Press, 1970). When the first edition of this innocent work was published in 1942, it had to be withdrawn, presumably because it included references such as this to sexual prowess.

[12]Caoimhin O Danachair, *The Year In Ireland* (Cork: Mercier Press, 1972).

[13]E. E. Evans, *Mourne Country* (Dundalk: Dundalgan Press, W. Tempest, Ltd., 1951). Revised Edition, 1967.

[14]J. C. Beckett, *The Making of Modern Ireland* (London: Faber and Faber, 1966), p. 263.

[15]A. Toynbee, *A Study of History*, 1934, Vol. 2 (London: Oxford University Press), p. 100.

[16]This theme is developed in E. E. Evans, *The Personality of Ireland*, 1973.

[17]A. T. Lucas, "The Plundering and Burning of Churches in Ireland," *North Munster Studies*, ed. E. Rynne (Limerick: Thomond Archaeol. Soc., 1967), pp. 172-229.

[18]Giraldus Cambrensis, *The Topography of Ireland*, J. J. O'Meara, translator, (Dundalk: Tempest, 1951), p. 85.

[19]E. E. Evans, "Introduction to Lord George Hill," *Facts from Gweedore* (Belfast: Institute of Irish Studies, 1971), p. viii.

[20]This topic is discussed in O Danachair's *The Year in Ireland*.

[21]K. H. Connell, *Irish Peasant Society* (Oxford: Clarendon Press, 1968), Chapter 4.

[22]Ibid., p. 120.

[23]Maire MacNeill, *The Festival of Lúghnasa* (London: Oxford University Press, 1962).

NED LEBOW

# British Images of Poverty in Pre-Famine Ireland

ONE OF THE MORE interesting enigmas of Victorian culture was the fact that the British public held different attitudes toward poverty in Britain and in Ireland. As the British grew more sympathetic to the plight of their own poor, they maintained for the most part their ancient antipathy toward the paupers of Ireland.[1] Thus, while a variety of arguments were advanced in Parliament, the press, and the journals, suggesting that poverty at home was more the result of impersonal economic factors than of personal moral deficiencies, the same sources of opinion became even more convinced that poverty in Ireland was the fault of the Irish themselves. What accounts for this perceptual discrepancy? What functions did it fulfill?

All societies develop moral codes to regulate social behavior. Members of a society are more or less imperfectly socialized into accepting the validity of these ethical imperatives and into conforming to the behavioral norms estab-

Ned Lebow, Editor and Co-author of *Divided Nations in a Divided World* and author of the forthcoming *Between Peace and War: The Anatomy of International Crisis*, is Assistant Professor of Political Science at the City University of New York, and Research Associate of the Institute of War and Peace Studies, Columbia University. Professor Lebow has published numerous articles on Irish politics, Middle Eastern history, and communal conflict. He is political editor of the Irish-American journal, *Sword of Light*. Portions of "British Images of Poverty in Pre-Famine Ireland" have appeared in Lebow's *White Britain and Black Ireland* (Philadelphia: Institute for the Study of Human Issues, 1970).

lished by them. To the extent that an individual internalizes such a moral code, it becomes difficult for him consciously to violate it without suffering guilt or anxiety. Psychologists have suggested that repeated violations of important elements of internalized moral codes can produce intolerable anxiety or "dissonance," which must be reduced if the individual is to continue to function effectively.[2]

Such anxiety can be reduced in two ways: by stopping the anxiety-producing behavior or, if that is impossible, by attempting to rationalize into harmony the discrepancy between the values and the behavior. The most common rationalizations attempt to redefine the significance of the behavior and hence, to justify it. Thus, in a recent article in the *New York Times* on the rise of juvenile crime, a young black gang leader argued that his "rip offs" were justifiable because white affluence is the result of exploitation of blacks and, moreover, whites were too rich to really miss the loss.[3]

Social stereotypes can also serve to reduce such dissonance. Harold Isaacs, in his *Images of Asia,* suggests that the stereotype of the "faceless" Chinese was developed by Europeans in response to the horrible suffering they observed (and indeed, helped to produce) in China. The stereotype, which incorporated the belief that the Chinese were inured to suffering, unmindful of poverty, and generally content with their lot, helped Westerners to overcome the great uneasiness and even guilt they developed by reason of the disparity between their affluence and Chinese poverty.[4]

It can be argued that Western colonial empires produced such dissonance because the basic tenets of Christianity and later, of liberal political culture, ran counter to the political, economic, and social exploitation with characterized modern colonialism. For a variety of political and economic reasons, colonizers were unwilling to renounce voluntarily the advantages they derived from the exploitation of the colonial population, and throughout the nineteenth century found an increasing need—especially in light of the growing attacks on colonial practices by reformers at home—to harmonize the contradictions between the accepted values of the metropolitan society and the actual practices of colonial rule. (The stereotype of the native functioned to fulfill this need.)

Students of colonialism have suggested that colonizers have attributed remarkably uniform characteristics to the peoples they came to dominate. With almost monotonous regularity, they described colonial natives as indolent and self-complacent, cowardly but brazenly rash, violent, superstitious and incapable of hard work. On the more complimentary side, they were described as hospitable, good-natured, and curious but incapable of prolonged attention. Of all these characteristics, indolence appears to be the trait most universally ascribed to the natives, and Albert Memmi, a student of French colonialism, writes that "it seems to receive the unanimous approval of all colonizers from Liberia to Laos, via the Maghreb."[5] Unless colonial natives were by nature universally lazy—an unlikely supposition—we must conclude that colonizers projected this trait upon the colonized by reason of their own psychological and political need for such an image. By defining themselves as hardworking, thrifty, and honest, and the natives as indolent, superstitious, and lacking purpose, the colonial elite, who profited from the *status quo,* could shift the burden of responsibility for the disparity between their affluence and the natives' poverty from themselves to the natives. The rationalization permitted them to counter the arguments of their opponents, reduce internal guilt and anxiety and accordingly enjoy the profits of colonial exploitation.

Nowhere was the discrepancy between the condition of the colonizers and colonized so great or so apparent as in

nineteenth-century Ireland. Over the centuries, British colonizers had expelled the native Irish from their land, deprived them of their political rights, and attempted to make
them subservient to British interests. The periodic uprisings
of the Irish gave rise to brutal policies designed to secure the
ascendancy of the Anglo-Irish elite. The accumulative effect
of such measures—Cromwellian attempts at genocide,
widescale appropriation of estates, the Penal Laws and,
later, the widescale evictions of peasants—had reduced the
mass of the native Irish to a level of poverty unrivaled
elsewhere in Europe. At the same time, the minority of
settlers, administrators, and soldiers who represented British power had achieved a relatively high degree of prosperity. By the nineteenth century, there were in fact two
Irelands: one Protestant, Anglo-Scottish, prosperous and
politically influential; the other, Catholic, Irish, and living on
the edge of starvation. Authorities as diverse as John Stuart
Mill, Alexis de Tocqueville and the Duke of Wellington—an
Irish peer—declared the condition of the Irish to be worse
than that of the poorest Indian peasant or North African
*fellahin*. William Thackeray, who visited Ireland in 1843, felt
compelled to warn his compatriots to keep away from that
unhappy country:

> The traveler is haunted by the face of popular starva-
> tion. It is not the exception, it is the condition of the
> people. In this fairest and richest of countries, men are
> suffering and starving by the millions. . . . The epi-
> curean, and traveler for pleasure, had better travel
> anywhere than here; where there are miseries that one
> does not dare to think of; where one is always feeling
> how helpless pity is, and how helpless relief, and is
> perpetually ashamed of being happy.[6]

The fact that Ireland was an economic disaster was well

known throughout Britain. Unlike other colonies which were distant from the metropole, populated by cultures that spoke foreign tongues and had little intercourse with the British public, Ireland was no further than several hours sea voyage away; her people spoke English and had had a long and intimate relationship with Britain. Irishmen, unable to find employment at home, populated the burgeoning urban slums of Glasgow, London, and the Midlands, and Irish spokesmen sat in the Parliament at Westminster. Supported by a small but influential coterie of British sympathizers, they lashed out at imperial injustice and carefully documented the conditions of the mass of the Irish people. The most striking documentation was actually supplied by the opposition. In 1843, Robert Peel—known as "Orange Peel" to the Irish—authorized a Royal Commission to investigate the causes of violence in Ireland. The "Devon Commission," as it came to be known, solicited testimony from several hundred witnesses and submitted its report to Parliament in 1845. Much to the chagrin of the Tory Government, the Commission attributed the widespread violence to the appalling poverty of the peasantry, which was carefully documented in the study. This poverty, in turn, was traced to the short-sighted policies of the landowning class and, in particular, to their refusal to extend to their tenantry any of the elementary legal safeguards which were commonplace in England. The Commission criticized the successive administrations which had fostered and maintained the arbitrary prerogatives of these landlords.[7]

The reaction to the findings of the Devon Commission and other contemporary pleas for reform was very revealing. Unable or unwilling to cope with the magnitude of the Irish problem, the overwhelming majority of parliamentarians, journalists, and economists rejected the conclusions of the Commission and continued to rely upon the traditional moral explanation for Irish poverty despite all the accumulating and compelling evidence to the contrary. It is striking to note that the very newspapers and journals that argued that poverty in Britain was largely the result of impersonal economic forces still insisted that poverty in Ireland was almost entirely the result of the morally deficient nature of the Irish people.

By far the most important organ of public opinion in mid-century Britain was *The Times*, which aspired to the role of spokesman for the British nation. While claiming to mold public opinion, *The Times* in reality pursued a cautious policy during the early years of Victoria's reign and, more often than not, reflected rather than formed elitist opinion. Speaking of *The Times*, the *Edinburgh Review* exclaimed: "It takes up no failing cause, fights no uphill battle, advocates no great principle, holds out a helping hand to no oppressed or obscure individual—it is ever strong upon the stronger side."[8] While such partisanship was biased, it did strike at an elemental truth about *The Times*, the very characteristic that makes it an ideal source by which to gauge middle and upper class opinion on the question of poverty.

*The Times* was sympathetic to the condition of the English poor. Her leader writers pilloried the view that British poverty was primarily the result of personal moral failings. In 1844, for example, the newspaper declared:

> Poverty is tortured and disciplined [in England] . . . upon the express assumption that it is not that stern, overpowering necessity which, do what we will, we cannot altogether root out or overcome!—no—but that it is in every case self-caused, and may therefore safely be treated as a condition from which the sufferer has the *power*, if he had only the will, to escape.[9]

*The Times* insisted that poverty was largely the result of

economic fluctuations and accordingly suggested that the state bore some responsibility toward those who were reduced to penury by forces beyond their control. Several editorials during the "hungry forties" lauded the creation of private charities to aid the poor and urged readers to subscribe to them. By way of contrast, *The Times*, at the height of the great Irish potato famine, discouraged private charities from contributing to the relief of distress in that country.

Such differences in policy—hardly unique to *The Times*—derived from differing perceptions of the causes of poverty in the two countries. For in Ireland, *The Times* advanced the very explanation for poverty which it held as indefensible with respect to Britain. The newspaper declared the root cause of Ireland's woes to be the "proverbial lassitude" of the Irish people. Contrasting the hardworking and thrifty Englishman to the lazy Celt, the newspaper asked: "What is an Englishman made for but work? What is an Irishman made for but to sit at his cabin-door, read O'Connell's speeches and abuse the English?" Unlike the English, who were willing to work long hours for a meager return, the Irish, according to *The Times*, "can act and do work well, if they see the prospect of immediate advantage before them, but if the advantage be remote or doubtful, or, it be only the probability of increased comfort, then they appear to want energy. . . ."[10]

The Irishman's failure to develop a sustained sense of purpose appeared to anger *The Times* even more than his supposed indolence. Criticizing a speech by Daniel O'Connell in August 1843, the editors exclaimed:

We have believed, and our belief has been confirmed by the repeated declarations of Irishmen themselves, that if there was one single quality in which they were more deficient than another, it was fixedness of purpose and steadiness of action; that if there was one great radical fault in their moral constitution it was the volatility which prevented them from attempting or carrying out any work which required severity of application and intensity of purpose.[11]

Readers of *The Times* were fed a steady diet of "evidence" in support of these views by the newspaper's Irish correspondents, who portrayed the native Catholic Irish as ignorant, indolent, and scheming but totally irrational. One such dispatch, typical of the numerous Irish reports appearing in the newspaper thoughout the 'forties, informed readers that

> A more strange mixture than your genuine Irishman it is difficult to conceive. No man will haggle more for 6d., will part with money when he has it with less facility or be more backward to lay out any sum for any useful or profitable object whatever. He is great at a hard bargain, still greater at a job when he supposes he has effectually "done" you. He will take as much pains and resort to as many devices to win 5' by a job as would win him 50£ by straight forward enterprise. Yet, with all this hardfistedness, he will blindly agree to pay cent.per cent. for the loan of money, which if he *pays* will bring him to ruin.[12]

The correspondent took no note of the well-known fact, later documented by the Devon Commission, that when the peasant's crop failed, he often had no means of warding off starvation for himself and his family short of borrowing money at exorbitant rates of interest.[13] *The Times* "Commissioner" in Ireland, the doyen of the press community, was only slightly more understanding: "I have never concealed the virtues of the Celtic race. Their capacity for long endurance, their easy tractability of disposition, and their contentment with almost any loss, are virtues which the English people have not. The Englishman is patient, forbearing; but he is well used, and I never met with a contented Englishman." While the Englishman was ambitious and hence, never content, the Irishman, the "Commissioner" explained, was content and "endures oppression and he has therefore been oppressed and hardly used." Drawing logical—if perverse—conclusions from these assumptions, the "Commissioner" argued that the English should not be criticized for exploiting the Irish but, rather, the Irish ought to be blamed for tempting the English to oppress them![14]

"Paddy" received no better treatment on the editorial page. Here the dispatches of the "Commissioner" and the other Irish reporters were frequently cited in support of the contention that the Irish had only themselves to blame for their economic and political difficulties. In a leader dated May 15, 1844, the newspaper declared: "It is by industry, toil, perseverence, economy, prudence, by self-denial, and self-dependence, that a state becomes mighty and its people happy. . . . It is because the people of Ireland *generally* do not *labour* either physically or mentally, in anything like the proportion that the people of England do, that they are not generally near so wealthy."[15]

The views of *The Times* were echoed in the *Illustrated London News*, independent but Whig in sympathy, and by the Tory press. Peelite papers, like the *Herald,* the *Standard,* and the *Morning Post,* were even more vindictive in their verbal abuse of the Irish character. Among the significant London dailies, only the *Morning Chronicle,* a Whig organ of free trade and moderate reform, accepted the findings of the Devon Commission as justified. Relying on the insightful analysis of John Stuart Mill, the *Chronicle* urged Parliament to implement land reform and to curtail severely the arbitrary powers of the landlords.

The popular journals were no less certain that Irishmen were responsible for their own suffering. Contributors to *Blackwood's* and *Fraser's Magazine* advanced one set of arguments to explain poverty in Britain and quite another to explain the same phenomenon in Ireland. Without exception, they attributed the penury of Ireland to the indolence, short-sightedness, and fickle nature of her native inhabitants. One contributor to *Fraser's*, revelling in the superiority of the English over the Irish, declared:

> The English people are naturally industrious—they prefer a life of honest labour to one of idleness. They are a persevering as well as energetic race, who for the most part comprehend their own interests perfectly, and sedulously pursue them. Now of all the Celtic tribes, famous everywhere for their indolence and fickleness as the Celts everywhere are, the Irish are admitted to be the most idle and most fickle. They will not work if they can exist without it. Even here in London, though ignorant declaimers assert the reverse, the Irish labourers are the least satisfactory people in the world to deal with.[16]

*Punch* provides an even more striking example of this two-track reasoning. The magazine was merciless in its scorn for those who believed that British poverty was primarily the result of moral weakness or depravity. As the "hungry forties" in Britain progressed, *Punch* grew even more strident in tone.[17] The magazine opened its pages to moving descriptions of the conditions of "destitute but honest" workingmen and condemned the Government for not repealing the corn laws and initiating other action likely to reduce their distress.

*Punch,* the self-appointed spokesman of the English poor, ridiculed the cause of the Irish paupers in a most inhumane manner. "Mr. Punch" declared the Irish to be, by their very nature, the laziest and dirtiest people in all of Europe, if not the world. "Irishmen," he informed the readers, were "the sons and daughters of generations of beggars. You can trace the descent in their blighted, stunted forms—in their brassy, cunning, brutalized features." Their houses and huts were "monuments to national idleness," while the Irish themselves were "the missing link between the gorilla and the Negro." If the Irish were poor, they had only themselves to blame for their unenviable situation.[18]

Thus, chronic self-indulgence, indolence, and laxity of purpose were the primary features of the British image of the Irish that proved useful in explaining the existence of widescale poverty in Ireland. Other traits, such as their proverbial love of whiskey, abyssmal ignorance—attributed to their enslavement by Catholic superstition—and their inability to live for anything but the present were also enlisted to shift the burden for Irish ills from British to Irish shoulders. It rarely occurred to reporters, leader writers, or political commentators that some of the behavior they found so galling and difficult to comprehend might be the result and not the cause of poverty.

Concomitant with the almost universal belief that the Irish were responsible for their poverty was the equally prevalent assumption that the Irish, unlike their British neighbors, did not really mind their penury. This belief, which assumed that the Irish peasant was more animal than human, had a long history.

For centuries, travelers had noted with surprise the apparent contentment of the Irish despite the filth and poverty which surrounded them. William Lithgow, a renowned seventeenth-century traveler, compared the Irish unfavorably to the most backward of the Levant:

True it is, to make a fit comparison, the Barbarian

moore, the moorish Spaniard, the Turke, and Irishman, are the least industrious, and the most sluggish livers under the sunne, for the vulgar Irish I protest, live more miserably in their brutish fashion than the undaunted or untamed Arabian, the devilish-idolatrous Turcuman, or the moon-worshipping Caramans: shewing thereby a greater necessity they have to live, than any pleasure they have or can have in their living.[19]

Later travelers formed a similar impression. Richard Twiss, who toured Ireland in 1775, quoted Lithgow's description in support of his own contention.[20] Phillip Luckombe, a contemporary of Twiss, was equally amazed at the apparent good nature and cheerfulness of the natives despite their poverty. The squalor of Dublin and environs and the seemingly happy state of its inhabitants led him to speculate that the Irish must be racially distinct from the rest of mankind:

In general the outskirts of Dublin consist chiefly of huts, or cabbin, constructed of mud dried, and mostly without either chimney or window; and in these miserable kind of dwellings, far the greater part of the inhabitants of Ireland linger out a wretched existence. A small piece of ground is generally annexed to each, whose chief produce is potatoes; and on these roots and milk the common Irish subsist all the year round. . . . What little the men can earn from their labour, or the women by their spinning, is generally consumed in whiskey. . . . Shoes and stockings are seldom worn by these beings *who seem to form a different race from the rest of mankind;* their poverty is far greater than that of the Spaniards, Portuguese, or even Scotch peasants; notwithstanding which, they wear the appearance of content.[21]

Victorian observers were led to similar conclusions. Dr. Duncan, a Liverpool physician who studied the Irish condition, concluded that "The Irish seem to be as contented amidst dirt and filth and close confined air, as in clear and airy situations. While other people would consider comforts, they appear to have no desire for [them]; they merely seem to care for that which will support animal existence."[22] Commenting on this phenomenon, James Page, a Scottish divine who toured Ireland in 1836, declared that it would be disastrous to extend any kind of poor relief to the Irish people. He reasoned that

> The poor Irish work merely for their support; for what can, at the lowest calculation, sustain life. That obtained, they sit down contentedly in their cabins, in the midst of filth, and wretchedness almost exceeding what the greatest stretch of an Englishman's imagination can conceive: For subsistence they will work, and that with cheerfulness. Beyond this their degraded condition does not permit them to pass. To hold out to such people a prospect of support . . . might prove injurious in the highest degree.[23]

Another contemporary declared:

> In an intercourse with the common people, a day, an hour, cannot pass without being struck by some mark of talent, some display of an imagination at once glowing and enthusiastic, or some touch of tender and delicate feeling. How strange it is, that such a people should be content to dwell in smoky hovels, when, if they chose to exert themselves and employ their energies, which I think they possess, their conditions might be improved! But they are generally happy; therefore why wish to alter their state?[24]

These impressions of travelers were picked up and elaborated upon by the major organs of public opinion in England. *Fraser's Magazine* expressed the hope that large-scale immigration into England by Irish laborers, by presenting them with a contrast between conditions in these two countries, would encourage them to develop a taste for the better things of life. By 1847, the magazine felt compelled to admit its error:

> Born in a cabin and reared to look with complacency on the bundle of rags which covers his person, and the mess of potatoes which fills his belly, the young Irish peasant never acquired a taste for higher things, and cannot therefore understand even here in England—where, by the way, his associations continue to be Irish still—that his interests and those of his employer are identical.[25]

Even more reprehensible, according to *Fraser's*, was the Irish hatred of anybody who was industrious and attempted to improve his fortune by hard work and initiative. The magazine could only suggest that it was England's duty to effect a "moral revolution" in Ireland.

Contributors to *Blackwood's* advanced the same thesis. They were convinced that the Irish were distinct from the human race. Writing in opposition to extending further relief to the Irish poor, one writer asserted: "The people are fond of coarse food, which we think unfit for men, but they prefer it . . . the Irish consider the use of 'bread and meat' an infliction." Therefore, he reasoned, "there is, in reality, neither that distress nor that scarcity which we are taught to believe exist there." Pushing the argument to its logical conclusion, he declared, "the real truth is . . . that though there is more squalid filth and raggedness in Ireland (for those are national tastes) there is much less real misery or distress in that country than exists in England."[26]

*The Times* insisted that Irish poverty had to be understood within an Irish context. Disclaiming any British responsibility for the depressed state of that country, the newspaper asked what could be done with people who preferred potatoes to bread and voluntarily chose to live in conditions that even their pigs would not tolerate. For *The Times*, the real problem was the inescapable fact that "The uncivilized habits of the Irish have made them callous to so much of their poverty as does not *press* upon them in the shape of actual hunger, and have therefore tended to perpetuate that poverty through successive generations."[27] Britain's mission was not to alleviate Irish distress but to civilize her people and teach them to feel and act like human beings.

It should be made clear that the dominant British image of Ireland demanded a rigid distinction between the "native Irish" and the "Anglo-Irish." The former were Catholic and described as Celtic; the latter, Protestant and of English or Scottish extraction. It was the Catholic Irish Celt who was the object of British scorn. The Anglo-Irishman was perceived to be an altogether different creature, one who exhibited all the sterling qualities that had made the British nation great. The well-known fact that the majority of Anglo-Irish were concentrated in Ulster, the most prosperous province of Ireland, was often cited by Englishmen as proof of the difference in quality between the two populations.

This argument, clear-cut and perhaps persuasive by reason of its simplicity, was also incorrect. The Devon Commission had reported that in southern Ireland, the land was poorly managed, minutely subdivided, and frequently rack-rented. More often than not, the peasant held no lease, and his rent sometimes exceeded the actual valuation of the land. Moreover, he had no security of tenure. In Ulster, the majority of farmers either owned their own land or were protected by the custom of "Ulster right," which guaranteed recompense to a tenant for improvements he had made upon the expiration of his lease. The Devon Commission concluded that these safeguards enabled the Catholic residents of Ulster who came under their protection to be almost as prosperous as their Protestant neighbors. Accordingly, they recommended that both the practice of Ulster right and long-term leases be extended throughout the country.[28]

The real distinction in Ireland was not between Saxon and Celt or between Protestant and Catholic but between those Irishmen protected by custom and law and those exposed to the arbitrary power of the landlords. Arthur Young, the famous agriculturalist, pithily summed up the difference when he exclaimed: "Give a man the secure possession of a bleak rock, and he will turn it into a garden; give him a nine-years' lease of a garden and he will convert it into a desert."[29] The Irish Catholic peasants of the south usually did not have even the dubious advantage of a nine-year lease.

Once again, despite all the evidence to the contrary, the differences between Ulster and the rest of Ireland suggested only the familiar answer to most Englishmen. In the words of one traveler:

> The visitor would observe that in the Protestant districts six days each week are dedicated to labour, and the sabbath dedicated to the offices of religion; whilst in other districts half the week is passed in idleness or dissipation of holidays, and the sabbath neglected. It is true that in the breasts of the Irish Catholics he will find a strong sense of religion, agreeable to their mode of faith and ceremony; but he will also find that these modes of faith and ceremony are subversive to the spirit of industry. . . .[30]

Nassau Senior, a prominent government economist,

drew an even more rigid distinction. For him, there were "two Irelands" which coexisted uneasily side by side:

> One is chiefly Protestant, the other is chiefly Roman Catholic. . . . The population of one is laborious but prodigal; no fatigue repels them—no amusement diverts them from the business of providing the means of subsistence and of enjoyment. . . . that of the other is indolent but parsimonious.[31]

The dichotomy of the lazy Celt and the industrious Saxon seemed very neat at first glance. However, there was one very serious difficulty with this model of Irish affairs: how to account for the behavior and reputation of the Irish landlords.

The Anglo-Irish proprietary class had long been the object of verbal abuse in England. Since the days of Elizabeth, they had been taken to task for their shortsighted and often cruel policies toward their tenantry. By the nineteenth century, the attacks had increased in response to both their harsh policies and social pretensions and even the friends of the Anglo-Irish establishment were no longer able to ignore them.

Nineteeth-century economists, following the lead of David Ricardo, devoted considerable attention to the land problem in Ireland. While divided in their analysis of the proper path toward economic development in Ireland, they nearly unanimously condemned the subdivision and rack-renting practiced by many landlords.[32] This condemnation was echoed in the press and in Parliament and, if the British public learned to view the Irish peasant as shiftless and lazy, they came to see Irish landlords as greedy, callous, profligate, and even cruel.

In the thirties and forties, the Irish landowning class came under increasing attack in Parliament. Both conserva-

tive gentry and Radical free-trader criticized rack-renting
and mass evictions. The Tories, reluctant to tamper with
property rights, demanded a moral reform of the Irish
proprietary class. The Radicals and the Irish Repealers, less
in awe of the "rights" of the landlords, urged a tax on
absentees and legislation to curb their arbitrary powers. The
consensus in Parliament proved to be against legislative
action but favored the creation of a commission to investigate the causes of rural distress in Ireland. The Devon Commission, the result of this agitation, created an even stronger
case for legislative action, which embarrassed the Tory
Government and its supporters.

Many English publicists carried their indignant zeal
against the landlords to the point that it became inconsistent
with their dichotomous view of the two Irelands. The Liberal and Radical publications, which attributed Ireland's poverty to the moral weakness of Celtic Irishmen, frequently
explained this behavior in terms of the failure of the landowning class to set a proper example. *Fraser's Magazine*, for
example, traced the moral deficiencies of the Irish peasant
to the policies of the landlords. The Irishman was lazy and
shortsighted, the magazine declared:

> . . . because the Irish labourer has never been encour-
> aged nor felt that it was his interest, to be industrious. A
> resident gentry, with estates mortgaged to the water-
> line, create of necessity, a pauperized tenantry, who, in
> turn, neglect and oppress the labourer—giving him, in
> lieu of wages, a miserable potato garden, and training
> him in that school of habits of practical deceit as well as
> theoretical lying. How can it be otherwise then that a
> people so circumstanced should be indolent, cunning,
> savage and chronically poor?[33]

Even *The Times*, the bulwark of defense for property

rights, attacked the Irish landlords for abusing their privileges. In 1843, the newspaper compared them to fickle and irresponsible despots, reaping all the advantages of their favored position without exercising any of its responsibilities. What Ireland needed, *The Times* declared, was "real charity and understanding on the part of the landlords toward the poor and impoverished tenants."[34]

By 1845, *The Times*—albeit cautiously—had come out in favor of legislation to limit the arbitary powers of the landlords. Like *Fraser's* and *Blackwood's*, *The Times* now depicted the self-indulgence, extravagance, heartlessness, and cupidity of the landlords as a major source of economic stultification in Ireland. The newspaper concluded that the contrast between the solicitude shown by English landlords toward their tenants and the callous disregard manifested by the Irish landlords toward their peasantry could only stem from their respective national characters. Ireland's evils were entirely the fault of Irishmen, landlords and peasants, who lacked the moral fiber that had made Britain great:

> The closer we examine [Ireland's] wants, the more do we become convinced that the misgovernment of which she complains is the misgovernment of her own sons. The landlords, for the most part, so misgovern their estates, that their tenantry are disheartened; and the tenantry almost universally so misgovern their farms, that they do not produce one-third of the produce which they are capable; while all unite in so misgoverning the natural capabilities of the country, that instead of being, as she ought to be, the richest and most prosperous, she is the poorest and most neglected country in Europe.[35]

Thus, the major organs of public opinion in Britain

ascribed the poverty of Ireland to the moral deficiencies of the native Irish. This was, after all, the major thrust of the British defense against Irish accusations, that her poverty was the result of centuries of exploitation and oppression by Britain. Yet, to account for the behavior of the Irish landlords—who were, for the most part, Anglo-Irish—British journals, newspapers, and parliamentarians imputed to them all the traits commonly ascribed to the native Irish. The characterization of the Irish landowning class, similar in practically every respect to that of the peasants, violated the first premise of the stereotype by contradicting the firmly drawn distinction between Saxon and Celt.

Many newspapers and journals caught up on this logical dilemma simply ignored it. Others attempted to circumvent the difficulty by completely disregarding the well-documented fact that most of the Irish landlords were not "Irish" but Anglo-Irish or even English. Reference after reference, several of which have already been quoted, depicted the Irish landlord as "native Irish" and explained his behavior in terms of his ethnic character.

Most Irish proprietors were in fact either descendants of Cromwellian adventurers or British capitalists who had invested in Irish property. They were not Irish in culture, religion, or political association. The small number of landlords who were "native Irish" were often regarded as among the best proprietors in the country, while the absentee landlords—the worst offenders in everybody's eyes—were almost entirely non-Irish. A great percentage of them had never even set foot in Ireland and had hired managers to oversee their estates and extract for them a yearly income. Nevertheless, many British observers explained the irresponsible behavior of these landlords in terms of their Irish character.

This seeming ability of British commentators on Ireland to ignore the obvious realities of Ireland in order to attribute its ills to the moral failings of the Irish character certainly appears to be indicative of a compelling need to disclaim any British responsibility for the state of Ireland. While it is the contention of this paper that this need was primarily psychological—occasioned by the glaring discrepancies between the growing affluence of Britain and the increasing pauperization of Ireland—it must not be overlooked that the stereotyped image of the Irish could also have functioned as a clever but conscious rationalization employed by special interests to justify and defend the *status quo* in Ireland.

Several important interest groups stood to profit from the acceptance of this view of Ireland. One might expect that the Anglo-Irish establishment quite consciously employed the stereotype to discredit assaults on their nearly arbitrary power. The Irish landowning class, under heavy attack by reformers in Britain, doubtless felt this need acutely. The Church of Ireland also had a vested interest in the image. Fighting what it perceived to be an increasing rear-guard action to maintain its prerogatives and hence its revenue, the Church had much to gain by explaining Irish dissatisfaction and agitation in terms of the "immature" character of the people.

Finally, it has been argued that the major British manufacturers had an important stake in the Irish-*status quo*.[36] The colonial exploitation of Ireland created a drain of capital from that country which, in part, helped to finance British industrial development. The depressed state of Ireland also created a labor surplus, prompting large-scale emigration to Britain and, by creating a source of cheap labor, permitted British industrialists to drive down wages. By the 1840s, however, British capital was a surplus commodity, hence the increasing investment abroad, and the internal economic crisis in Britain had already created a sufficiently high level of unemployment among British laborers to depress wages quite dramatically. One would

expect that industrialists would be more interested in finding markets and hence in encouraging political and economic stability in Ireland. The parliamentary speeches by
representatives of manufacturing constituencies suggest
that they were not blind to this concern.

Certainly, the fact that certain groups might have bene-
fitted from a particular image or policy does not prove they
consciously embraced such an image or policy because it
advanced their interests. Nevertheless, we might expect that
such people were more or less predisposed to that point of
view and were probably the least likely to be easily weaned
from it. Without examining individual motives, a difficult
task at best, the image of the indolent and childlike Celt
must have been self-serving in a very conscious way.

However, looking at the other side of the question,
there is considerable evidence to suggest that for many
people the image was "innocent" in that they derived no
direct political or economic gain from it. In many cases it
actually appeared to run counter to their proclaimed self-
interest. The English liberals and Radicals who contributed
to the magazines and newspapers quoted in this study are a
case in point. *The Times, Fraser's Magazine,* the *Illustrated
London News,* and *Punch* had no vested interest in the *status
quo* in Ireland. Surely for *The Times,* the reverse was closer
to the truth. The newspaper favored imperial expansion and
economic growth, preaching military preparedness in the
face of the turbulence of continental politics, particularly in
the early 1840s. *The Times* itself admitted that the condition
of Ireland partially defeated these goals: the government
was forced to station a large garrison in that country and, in
time of crisis, could not depend on the loyalty of the
majority of the inhabitants. The newspaper saw Ireland as
the weakest link in Britain's chain of defenses, a land seeth-
ing with dissatisfaction and vulnerable to revolutionary
agitation promoted by Britain's enemies. Disturbed by this

state of affairs, *The Times* preached reconciliation and it was probably for this reason that her editors supported moves to curb the power of the landlords. *The Times,* therefore, had no need to embrace the stereotype of the Irish for self-serving reasons, yet it saw no contradiction in attacking the Irish gentry while continuing to analyze Irish affairs in terms of the stereotyped image of the indolent Celt. It simply reconciled its politics with its stereotypes by describing the proprietary class in terms of native characteristics, as if they had assimilated them over the years by diffusion or breathed them in with the heady Irish air.

The case of *Punch* is even more revealing. The magazine was usually in the forefront of reform: her editors favored the extension of the franchise, opposed most colonial adventures, and generally sided with the underdog. Yet, while the magazine sympathized with the plight of the British poor, it, too, explained Irish poverty in terms of the character of the natives. The same paradox can be said to hold true for a significant number of parliamentary Radicals who evidenced similar attitudes toward the Irish. Vociferous opponents of special privilege both at home and abroad, they nevertheless subscribed to the stereotyped image of the Celt, even when it could be said to be contradictory to their political interests.

Psychologists have suggested that the expectation of certain behavior evokes that very behavior in countless subtle ways. If a child is said to be stupid and is continually treated as such, it is unlikely, regardless of his native ability, that he will do well in school. If a man believes that his colleagues are hostile to him, he is likely to behave in such a defensive or insulting manner as to provoke true hostility. Stereotypes frequently involve a "self-fulfilling prophecy." Gordon Allport, reviewing the literature on prejudice, suggests that, "Too often we think of out-groups as simply possessing certain qualities and in-groups as having certain false images of these qualities. The truth of the matter is that these two conditions interact."[37] We can speculate that the image of the Irish, propagated for seven centuries, gradually became ever more a reality.

The major characteristics of the Irish treated in this paper have been their supposed indolence, laxity of purpose, and, to a lesser extent, their love of alcohol and their superstition. It is probably true that by the nineteenth century, the Irish displayed many of these characteristics more noticeably than did their English neighbors. The centuries of oppression had made it functional—both psychologically and economically—for them to behave in such a manner. One perceptive traveler, who visted Ireland in the latter half of the eighteenth century, observed:

> We keep the Irish dark and ignorant, and then we wonder how they can be so enthralled by superstition; we make them poor and unhappy, and then we wonder that they are so prone to tumult and disorder; we tie up their hands, so that they have no inducements to industry, and then we wonder that they are so lazy and insolent. No wonder that it should be part of the Irish character that they are so *careless for their lives,* when they have so little worth living for.[38]

If many Irish were indolent, they had been encouraged to be so. All too often, an Irishman who improved his land was either charged a higher rent or expelled to make room for a new tenant who would pay more for the land. John Stuart Mill, a lifelong crusader against the Irish land system, declared:

> Almost alone among mankind the cottier is in the condition that he can scarcely be any better or worse off by any action of his own. If he were industrious and

prudent, nobody but his landlord would gain; if he is lazy and intemperate, it is at his landlord's expense.[39]

If the Irish were superstitious, once again, British policy had helped to create the conditions under which ignorance flourished. The Penal Laws had forbidden Catholics to be educated abroad and had outlawed education for Catholics within Ireland. Centuries of persecution had lowered the intellectual level of the clergy but simultaneously strengthened the power of the religion over the people. The Church was their one remaining native institution; its very existence was an act of defiance to the alien conqueror. The power it came to wield derived in part from its treatment by the British Government. Struck by this irony, Richard Cobden suggested that the power of the Church would wane only when it became the established church.[40]

The same argument can be made with respect to the high incidence of alcoholism in Ireland. A population reduced to extreme poverty and given little hope of bettering its condition must inevitably seek some means of escape from the daily frustrations of life. The Victorian Irish and the English working class found their escape in alcohol. This further depressed their condition and permitted those seeking additional confirmation of the stereotype to deftly reverse cause and effect and explain poverty in terms of the moral depravity of the people.

What had begun as a largely fictitious image in the minds of the early British colonists in Ireland became ever more the social reality. Given such a situation, it is not difficult to see how the image of the indolent Celt could gradually have come to dominate the perceptions of Englishmen who had never set foot in Ireland and had no vested interest in the political and economic *status quo* of that country. Over the centuries, the image spread from Ireland to Britain with the steady stream of commentaries, travel descriptions, and reports written by colonists, administrators, and more casual visitors to Ireland. The image became incorporated in British histories of Ireland, political pamphlets, and newspaper reports. Englishmen were conditioned almost from the cradle to accept the stereotyped description of the native Irish as a reality. Socialized into accepting the validity of the image, those Englishmen who visited Ireland brought their preconceived notions with them and had little difficulty in finding confirmation of their beliefs. Their subsequent writing and conversations further reinforced the grip of the image upon the British mind. It is not difficult to see how by the nineteenth century, the image became something of a perceptual prison, a closed image through which information about Ireland was structured and given meaning and, perhaps, an image in terms of which policy was formulated.

The effect of this socialization process was strengthened by the continuing existence of the conditions that had made the image necessary in the first place. The economic condition of the mass of the Irish people, rather than improving, deteriorated dramatically in the first half of the nineteenth century. In the decade prior to the great potato famine, the decline of the availability of arable land, the population explosion—itself a function of galling poverty—and the ensuing inflation of rents created even greater distress. As a result, the disparity between the condition of the Irish peasantry and the British middle class became even greater—and more apparent, because it was the topic of considerable parliamentary interest. Those British observers who did venture into Ireland were invariably appalled by the plight of the Irish, though their conclusions about the cause and cure varied considerably.

Unwilling to make any sacrifices to improve the condition of Ireland or honestly at a loss at how to cope with a problem of such magnitude, most middle and upper class

Britons, lacking Thackeray's painful honesty, preferred instead to dismiss the horrors of Ireland from their minds. They did so by defending the image of the indolent Celt who really did not mind his poverty despite the fact that his image was both logically inconsistent and contrary to the considerable evidence they had.

When British policy is examined in light of the stereotype, it becomes apparent that it was not entirely hypocritical. While self-interest and political expediency were often conscious elements of policy, it is probably also true that most members of the informational and decision-making elites did not perceive and could not allow themselves to recognize the contradiction between their image and the actual state of affairs in Ireland. Thus, while the British people condemned oppression and exploitation in other parts of the world, they remained blind to its existence in their own back yard. The sufferings of the Algerian *fellaheen,* Polish peasants and, later, Russian Jews, evoked the sympathy of the British public, but shielded by their stereotype, they remained relatively immune to the cries of the Irish. Such a lack of empathy could not but prove disastrous to the success of the Union.

[1]One cannot comment on British attitudes toward the Irish without noting the pioneering study of L. Perry Curtis Jr., *The Anglo-Saxons and Celts.* (Bridgeport, Conn.: The Conference on British Studies, 1968). Curtis links the advent of racist attitudes in Britain toward the Irish in the late nineteenth century to the rise of racism (primarily anti-Semitism) on the continent. He sees such racism as a function of industrial development. While it is true that the insecurities created by rapid economic and social change exacerbated anti-Irish feeling, especially among the working class, which had to compete for jobs with Irish immigrants, such

prejudice had deep historical roots and was hardly a new phenomenon. British racism was nothing novel but simply an expression of the age-old anti-Irish prejudice couched in terms of the jargon of the day. The purpose of this study is not to discredit Curtis but to propose an alternate hypothesis. My contention, that the roots of anti-Irish prejudice lie in an earlier period, is further documented in "Cambrensis to Macaulay: British Historians and Irish History," *Erie-Ireland*, December 1973.

²See, for example, Leon Festinger, *A Theory of Cognitive Dissonance* (Stanford: Stanford University Press, 1962); Leon Festinger, *et al.*, *Conflict, Decision, and Dissonance* (Stanford: Stanford University Press, 1964).

³*The New York Times*, November 2, 1971, Section 6, p. 27.

⁴Harold R. Isaacs, *Images of Asia: American Views of China and India* (New York: Capricorn Books, 1962), p. 99.

⁵Albert Memmi, *The Colonizer and the Colonized* (New York: Orion Books, 1965), p. 79.

⁶William Makepeace Thackeray, *The Irish Sketchbook* (New York: J. Winchester, 1844), p. 37. Published under the pseudonym M. A. Titmarsh.

⁷*Report from Her Majesty's Commissioners of Inquiry into the State of the Law and Practice with Respect to the Occupation of Land in Ireland*. Parliamentary Papers, H. C., 1845 (605), XIX; *Evidence Taken Before Her Majesty's Commissioners of Inquiry into the State of the Law and Practice with Respect to the Occupation of Land in Ireland*. Parliamentary Papers, H. C., 1845 (606), XIX; (616), XXI; (657), XXI. (Hereafter referred to as the *Devon Commission*.)

⁸*Edinburgh Review*, XXXVII (May 1823), 364.

⁹*The Times*, January 17, 1844, p. 4.

¹⁰Ibid., January 26, 1847, p. 6; September 3, 1845, p. 7.

¹¹Ibid., August 4, 1843, p. 4.

¹²Ibid., October 25, 1845, p. 8.

¹³*Devon Commission, Evidence, Part II*, p. 268.

¹⁴*The Times*, October 25, 1845, p. 8.

¹⁵Ibid., May 15, 1844, p. 6, and February, 26, 1846, p. 6.

¹⁶*Fraser's Magazine*, XXXVI (March 1847), 373.

¹⁷See, for example, *Punch*, II (1842), 195.

¹⁸Ibid., XIV (1849), 54; XVII (1851), 26 and 231.

¹⁹William Lithgow, *Description of Ireland and the Irish, A. D. 1619*, quoted in Richard Twiss, *A Tour in Ireland in 1775* (London: J. Robson, 1776), p. 152.

²⁰Ibid.

²¹Philip Luckombe, *A Tour Through Ireland* (London: T. Lowndes & Son, 1783), p. 19.

²²Dr. Duncan of Liverpool, quoted in an anonymous pamphlet, *Observations of the Habits of the Labouring Classes in Ireland. . . .* (Dublin: Milliken and Son, 1836), p. 9.

[23]James Page, *Ireland: Its Evils Traced to their Source* (London: R. B. Seeley & W. Burnside, 1836), p. 113.

[24]Henrietta G. Chatterton, *Rambles in the South of Ireland* (London: Saunders and Olley, 1839), p. 113.

[25]*Fraser's Magazine*, XXVI (March 1847), 373.

[26]*Blackwood's Magazine*, LIX (March 1846), 600 and 602.

[27]*The Times*, December 8, 1843, p. 4.

[28]*Devon Commission, Report*, p. 14.

[29]Quoted by William Bridges, *Plantation of Ireland, Three Practical Suggestions for the Colonization and Re-organization of Ireland* (London: H. Baccliere, 1849), pp. 12-13.

[30]Thomas Walford, *The Scientific Tourist Through Ireland . . . by an Irish Gentleman* (London, 1818), pp. 6-7.

[31]Nassau William Senior, *Journals, Conversations and Essays Relating to Ireland* (London: Longmans, Green & Co., 1868), I, 212.

[32]See R. D. Collison Black, *Economic Thought and the Irish Question, 1817-1870* (Cambridge University Press, 1962), pp. 15-86.

[33]*Fraser's Magazine*, XXVI (May 1847), 575.

[34]*The Times*, January 31, 1843, p. 4.

[35]Ibid., October 4, 1845, p. 5.

[36]See Eric Strauss, *Irish Nationalism and British Democracy* (New York: Columbia University Press, 1951).

[37]Gordon Allport, *The Nature of Prejudice* (Cambridge: Addison-Wesley, 1955), p. 156.

[38]Thomas Campbell, *A Philosophical Survey of the South of Ireland* (Dublin, 1778), p. 253.

[39]John Stuart Mill, *England and Ireland* (London: Longmans, Green, Reader and Dyer, 1868), II, 283.

[40]Richard Cobden, *England, Ireland & America* (London: P. Brown, 1836).

JAMES MACKILLOP

# Finn Mac Cool:
# The Hero and the Anti-Hero
# in Irish Folk Tradition

ONE OF THE DISTINCTIONS of the Irish national resurgence of the last century was the widespread fascination, both popular and scholarly, with the country's unique ancient tradition of poetry, narrative, and myth. There was nothing in itself distinctive about a revival of the most flattering traditions of one's own country; this was a part of national movements everywhere. In Germany especially the movement for national unity was warded by a legion of fastidious scholars and at least one titanically egotistical artist who wrote music-dramas. What set the Irish example apart from the general European pattern is that—despite all odds against it—the tradition of the ancient past had never died. Irish intellectuals and artists, like their counterparts abroad, may have needed to revive or invent a tradition for their country for themselves, but the mass of the Irish people did not. Even in the areas of the island where the native language was no longer spoken, Irishmen knew their own tradition and culture to be something quite different from that of the English and Anglicized overclass which oppressed them. And of all the characters of ancient tradition the one who

James MacKillop is Associate Professor of English at Onondaga Community College (SUNY). He has published critical articles in Canadian and American learned journals, and he is presently compiling a dictionary of Celtic mythology and a gloss of Irish-in-English usage.

was the most alive to the Irish peasant of 1800-1916 was Finn MacCool.[1]

The literature of the distant past has, at least since the time of Sir Walter Scott, been looked upon by most modern readers as romantic, fantastic, and wholly divorced from the contemporary world. Further, many contemporary readers, especially Americans, tend to look upon all traditional literature recorded since the fall of the Roman Empire as "folklore." Irish tradition cannot be categorized so easily.

Certainly in Irish tradition we find much that resembles what we usually call "folklore": hyperbolic detail, expression of wish, etc.; and the majority of Irish narratives can be classified in Aarne and Thompson's famous motif-index. Nevertheless, Irish tradition, as the great Norwegian scholar Reidar Th. Christiansen noted long ago, is not comparable to what is called folklore elsewhere. The reasons for this, which have been argued quite well for the past two generations by men like Christiansen, T. F. O'Rahilly, and Gerard Murphy, are that Irish traditions find their roots in the pre-Christian religions of the Celtic people, that for many centuries these traditions were kept alive by a learned class of professional poets and storytellers, and, third, that these traditions were believed by many people—learned and unlettered alike—to be the genuine history of an oppressed people dispossessed of their land. In short, many of the Gaelic peasants of 1800-1916 would take violent umbrage at our looking upon Finn MacCool as anything other than an ancient—but highly reliable—champion of his people. In 1857 the great scholar and translator Standish Hayes O'Grady wrote of coming upon a laborer in a field discussing *ex cathedra* on the laws and weapons of the Fianna of Finn MacCool.[2] About the same time Campbell of Islay reported that the Gaelic speaking Highlanders mentioned the Fenian heroes with as much feeling and sympathy and belief in their existence as readers of the newspapers did of the British Army in Crimea.[3] An understanding of Finn MacCool, we may therefore surmise, is not simply the rummaging of fossilized cultural arcana but rather an approach to the mind of the Irish peasant in his everyday life.

The narratives of Finn MacCool and his Fianna are at the center of one of the four cycles of traditional Irish literature. Two of the other cycles, the Mythological and the Ulster or Red Branch, appear to be of older origin, perhaps dating in chronicle as early as the fourth century. The remaining cycle, called by Myles Dillon the "Cycle of Kings," appears to be based on actual historical figures and is of later composition, and has been delineated only in our times.[4] The third cycle, Finn's cycle, has been the most popular of all, so much so that different parts of it have gone under different names over the years. The name we shall use here is "Fenian," although many scholars would reject this, not only for the now slightly dated political associations but more because the word "Fenian" is of modern coinage. Like the literature of the other three cycles, Fenian narratives are first divided in two classes according to the way in which they reach us. Older manuscripts which appear to have come almost exclusively from lettered composers center on Finn MacCool himself, although they allow his character a wide range of expansion. According to texts dating from as early as the twelfth century, Finn and the bulk of his men died at the battle of Gabhra, which according to highly unreliable chronicle was in A.D. 283. Narratives from the cycle may be called "Fenian," but many scholars in the past have called them "Finnian" to denote the dominance of the hero. Another body of tales about the same heroes has been recorded from oral sources. In many cases, especially closer to modern times, "oral sources" meant illiterate peasants from the *Gaeltacht*, but it has not always meant so; from the twelfth century to at least the beginning of the eighteenth, Gaelic story tellers were chiefly from a professional class, "unlettered," perhaps, but without the pejorative flavor that the word has in an era of compulsory literacy. Because these narratives are usually told in a retrospective frame in which Finn's son has survived from heroic times and must explain the older tradition to Saint Patrick, they are called "Ossianic," from the Highland form of Oisín, which is better known in English. Both Fenian traditions, manuscript and oral, comprise a vast number of narratives, but what is more important, both also comprise an immense number of texts. The bulk of Fenian materials from both written and oral traditions is a much more substantial body than survives from any of the other cycles. Despite the fashion for Cúchulainn and other Ulster figures among the generation of writers in the Yeatsian Irish Renaissance, Finn and his Fianna had long since surpassed all of the characters of all other cycles in the affections of the Irish peasantry. Apart from the literati, few Irishmen today can speak of such figures as Deirdre, Conchobhar mac Nessa, Lugh Lamhfada, but nearly every living Irishman and many Irish Americans, know at least a fragment of narrative about Finn MacCool.

What do Irishmen, few of whom would care to call themselves "peasants," know about Finn MacCool from tradition? They see him as a giant, a great defender of his people, a hunter, a storyteller. One of the best-known stories has him rip out a divot of turf in Ulster and throw it into the sea, thus creating Lough Neagh and the Isle of Man at the same time. He started to build the Giant's Causeway, but got distracted and did not finish. Further, most Irishmen see an allusion to Finn in the name of de Valera's party, the Fianna Fail, as the best known fianna or private militia from tradition is certainly Finn's. We can also find stories which do not accord at all with such a personality. Sometimes Finn is seen as a great blow-hard who talks too much. Often the mature Finn is described as taking an unwholesome interest in a

much younger lady, Grainne, and of being involved treach-
erously in the death of the young lady's lover. Most curious
of all is a story most often seen in children's collections in
which the national hero quails in fear when he is told that a
rival giant is eager to challenge him and thus runs home so
that his wife can ward off the invader with a clever trick. In
short, one often finds an unheroic or anti-heroic Finn existing side by side with the hero. Such a juxtaposition is, in fact,
a commonplace in more formal western literature. The most
curious aspect of this coexistence of the hero with the anti-
hero is that Finn often seems to be the projection of the
collective imagination of an angry, determined people in
search of their national liberation. The two Finns are coeval
in tradition, a paradox which Joyce plays with all through
*Finnegans Wake.* But Joyce was a cosmopolite who had no
special need for sustenance from Irish tradition; our an-
nounced concern is with the Irish peasantry: How could the
people who abandoned Parnell have tolerated such an apparent contradiction in their mythical national hero?

To approach the paradox of Finn's character within the
chronological limits of this series of essays, we might consider what was known about the hero in 1800, and who knew it;
and what was known about him in 1916, and who knew that.
The first questions are easier to answer, in part because of
the massive European ignorance of the Celtic past which has
been the subject of much commentary. One hardly needs to
survey all of Western literature previous to 1800 to demonstrate that no one but the Irish knew of Finn MacCool and
his fianna; we simply take judicial note of it. The only non-
Gaelic citations of the Finn that one may find are in the
histories and pseudo-histories of Ireland and Scotland. The
ill-informed amateur scholarship that surrounded the publication of James Macpherson's *Fingal* (1762), a name drawn
from Highland Gaelic Fenian ballads, is more positive proof
of non-Irish ignorance. What the Irish- or Gaelic-speaking

peasant knew about Finn is more difficult to measure as the narratives were kept alive only in oral tradition, a vast body of literature which was to be recorded gradually and incompletely over the next century. To assert that the records of mid- and late-century can speak for 1800 is to take issue in the continuing dispute over the permanence of oral tradition, but the overwhelming bulk of surviving texts, from both manuscript and oral traditions, indicates that the dominant mode of characterization of Finn MacCool was heroic until well into the nineteenth century.

The key to our understanding of Irish tradition in the early nineteenth century is "peasantry," no matter how distasteful the term is to contemporary, Republican Irishmen. By the end of the eighteenth century, Irish was a written language for perhaps as few as five to six hundred people.[5] And to speak the native language of Ireland was to find oneself a dispossessed peasant in one's own country. Such had not been true only a few decades previous. The late-blooming Irish aristocracy of leaders like Hugh O'Neill had flourished only two centuries earlier. More importantly and more recently, the "Hidden Ireland," described in copious detail by Daniel Corkery, produced a great body of literature on ancient themes current during the late seventeenth and the early eighteenth century. Turlogh O'Carolan, perhaps the best known of all Gaelic musicians and song writers, died in 1728; he was known—more than just figuratively—as the "Last of the Bards." Though the aesthetic achievement of the literature from "Hidden Ireland" is a matter of some dispute, it was written for a cultivated, albeit declining, audience. The patrons of the "Last of the Bards" may have been outlaw lords with what appeared to be uncouth manners in Georgian Dublin; they were at least men of pretense. Accordingly, there seems to be substantial evidence that the bard, Carolan himself, was known to English-speaking residents of the Pale, including Jonathan

Swift.[6] The audience for Gaelic storytellers growing up in
the generation after the catastrophic defeat at Ballinamuck
(September 8, 1798) were more likely to be dispirited tenant
farmers. And as we Americans have found after a generation
of television, the cumulative expectations of a writer's audience often put limits on what he can produce.

The death of the last of the bards signaled an impoverishment of Irish tradition greater than that from any
political or military defeat. The significance of the end of
the learned or manuscript tradition in the Irish language and
in Irish mythology cannot be measured without entering
into the imbroglio that is mythological theory. In all traditional literature there is a qualitative difference between the
kinds of characterization and narrative which survive in
written and oral texts. The earliest commentators, such as
Herder and Heyne, who worked during the eighteenth
century and who worked almost exclusively with Greek
materials, saw the manuscript tradition as the more conservative, usually maintained by priests and learned scribes;
the oral tradition was more subject to change and, although
it occasionally paralleled what was to be found in written
texts, it was more likely to be different, not only in form but
in theme and motif. This much is easy to discern; the more
difficult question was: Which came first? and by implica-
tion, which had the greater authority and validity? J. G.
Herder and the Brothers Grimm found greater creative
vitality among the people, which, they felt, ultimately gave
materials to highly innovative individual artists. The opposite view is that oral tradition derives from learned tradition and that oral narratives are frequently only mutilations
of written narratives that had been current almost as long;
the most vocal partisans of this view in recent years have
been Hans Naumann and Lord Raglan. Because the Irish
vernacular is the oldest in Europe, and because the Irish
manuscript tradition dates from about the fifth century, and

further, because Irish oral tradition is especially rich, the manuscript versus oral tradition has been the subject of much controversy. Gerard Murphy addresses himself to the problem in his lengthly introduction to the third volume of *Duanaire Finn*, (1953)[7] in what is probably the most important critique of Fenian literature. Murphy demonstrates that the manuscript and the oral traditions have always existed side by side and that the archetype of Finn MacCool has always been the same in both; the traditions are distinguished only by their preference for different narratives. For example, the oral tradition has always preferred to portray Finn as a giant, and has perpetuated the stories about him as a giant, or has transformed him into a giant in other stories in which his size was not especially significant. Learned Irishmen, such as Geoffrey Keating in his famous *History* (*Foras Feasa ar Eirinn*, c. 1633) protested this, saying, rather soberly, that Finn was not of abnormal size compared to his contemporaries.[8] Because widespread, professional collecting of oral tradition did not begin until the nineteenth century, manuscript tales will always appear to be older, as many more older texts are available. Nevertheless, enough records of older oral tradition do survive to support Murphy's argument that at least some oral or folk narratives are older than the manuscript redactions of the same tales. Indeed, the manuscript redactions appear to be not only later than the oral versions but bowdlerized as well. Professor Murphy believed that the author of the manuscript heroic tale *Bruidhean Chaorthainn* ("The Rowantree Dwelling") edited the details in such a way as to help preserve—or shall we say restore—the dignity of Finn and his warriors.[9] And what coarse or untoward details could not be excised from the tale were attributed to Conán Maol ("the bald"), the comic-Thersites butt of many Fenian pranks.

If the unlettered Irish peasantry were the only body of people in 1800 who knew much about Finn MacCool, there were others on the horizon who were eager to learn; there were Anglo-Irish (the few members of the landlord class who were enlightened had immediate access to sources), foreigners, first the English and then in massive numbers the Germans, and later, as the century wore on, there were educated members of the Gaelic population, men whose learning in the face of great obstacles was itself an heroic undertaking. Such readers came forth not because of any great sympathy with the lot of the Irish peasant but rather because of a series of unrelated phenomena. Most important, probably, was an interest in the ancient past which characterized the romantic taste all over Europe; Irish narratives were old, predating the Renaissance. In more scholarly circles the hunger for the remote past produced waves of Gothic revivals. As the ancient Celts frequently lived in close association with the Goths, so, too, those who would revive the Gothic were to take on the Celts as well. The impulse which led scholars to translate *Beowulf* led another body of men to translate the *Táin bó Cuailnge* and the *Acallamh na Senórach*. But the most immediate spark came from a man who despised the Irish peasant, a Scots Highland Tory named James Macpherson who transmogrified several collections of Highland Gaelic ballads into something he finally called *The Poems of Ossian* (1760-63). Whatever else may be said about Macpherson, his poems attracted wide attention, chiefly outside the Celtic world; among his readers were: Napoleon, Goethe, Coleridge, Thomas Jefferson, Mendelssohn, James Fenimore Cooper, Henry David Thoreau, Johannes Brahms, and Matthew Arnold. Although he could barely read or write Gaelic, James Macpherson, supported by currents he could not perceive, struck a blow for Celtic scholarship. Although he called the hero "Fingal," he created a literary market for the heroic Finn MacCool.

In the very earliest days of the translations of Irish texts, the material which was most in demand was Fenian. Samuel Derrick with *The Battle of Lora* (1762) and Charles Wilson, *Poems Translated from the Irish Language* (1782), both with scant readership, had begun translating before the full impact of Macpherson had taken effect, but their interest was primarily in the Fenian tradition. Charlotte Brooke in her *Reliques of Irish Poetry* (1780) has at least three lengthy Fenian peoms, "Ode to Gaul, Son of Morni," "The Chase," and "Magnus the Great." Thomas Moore produced at least two poems with Fenian settings, "The Wine Cup is Circling" and "Dear Harp of My Country." Similarly, some of the earliest qualified Irish philologists, such as Theophilus O'Flanagan (1762-1814), worked with Fenian or Ossianic materials; however, as with *Beowulf*, scholars could not come forth with translations of the most important texts until the language, grammar, vocabulary, and rhetoric had been studied more fully. This was begun by the Germans with at least initial success fifty years before the founding of the Gaelic League. Significantly, the first great body of Irish translation to be published were the six volumes of *The Transactions of the Ossianic Society*, produced between 1854 and 1861. It is worth noting that these translators were men of Gaelic stock: Nicholas O'Kearney, Standish Hayes O'Grady, John O'Daly, and Owen Conellan.

Where did this leave the Irish peasant? Initially it barely touched him at all. Most Irish peasants had difficult enough time in staying alive by the 1850s and most probably could not read Irish let alone English. The translations of ancient heroic narratives apparently were directed toward groups other than the peasantry; of the considerable body of original works in English that were sparked by the translations, at least 120 titles, only a tiny fraction, perhaps fewer than five works, was written by authors of peasant background. The one application of heroic Fenian materials which most peasants could recognize and accept was the use of the very name "Fenian" for the I.R.B., alternately known as the "Irish Republican Brotherhood" and the "Irish Revolutionary Brotherhood." Even here the mythological allusion was not a peasant suggestion; the I.R.B. adopted "Fenian" in 1858 on the advice of the scholar John O'Mahony, who was living in New York at the time. One oddity in the word "Fenian" is that it is a nineteenth-century coinage and was rarely used until the I.R.B. adopted it. Other forms of the word which are better supported by etymology are *Fena* and *Feinne*. Yet, "Fenian" stuck, and its political associations come first to many people's minds, even today. What is most significant about the political conception of the heroic Finn is that it produced not one scrap of new literature of any kind. We can say rather confidently that there is not one published novel or play from the political Fenians which portrays the heroic Finn, and we may be fairly certain that there are no poems either. Most tellingly, there is not one reference to Finn MacCool in the movement's rallying songs such as those found in Stephens' *Fenian Songster* or *Fenian War Songs* (both 1866). Neither is there any mention of Finn in any of the great collections of popular ballads from the nineteenth century, though this may be less significant because political and mythological references of any kind are not common in Irish traditional narrative songs, an observation supported by Professor D. K. Wilgus in his contribution to this collection.[10]

In sum, it appears that the common Irish countryman knew of the heroic character of Finn MacCool largely through proverb, anecdote, and allusion. The most accessible sources for this information today are probably Lady Gregory's Kiltartan books, especially the *History Book* (1909) and the *Poetry Book* (1919).[11] Here we find that the peasants interviewed by Lady Gregory said,

Finn MacCumhail was a great man. Every hair of his head had the full strength of a man in it. He was a very nice man, with fair hair hanging down his back like a woman; a grand man he was. When he would chew his little finger he would know all things, and he understood enchantments as well.[12]

Lest the observer feel that a nationalist like Lady Gregory seeks only to find flattering themes in the peasant tradition, we should immediately point out that the same combination of bravery and gentility describes Finn elsewhere in Gaelic tradition, even as far away as the Highlands of Scotland. T.D. MacDonald devotes an entire chapter to the "Fingalians" in his *Gaelic Proverbs and Proverbial Sayings*,[13] most of which focus on the hero's strength, generosity, and fairness. For example:

> "Fuil mo nàmh cha d'dh'iarr mi riamh,
> Na'm bu mhiann iris falbh an sith."
> "The blood of my enemy I neer did seek,
> Were he but willing to depart in peace."

Or

> "Cha d'thug Fionn riamh blàr gun chumhan."
> "Fionn never fought a fight
> without offering terms."[14]

Similarly, the heroic narratives that were circulated in the nineteenth century were late redactions of tales that had been known for centuries. As the extensive bibliography in Alan Bruford's *Gaelic Folktales and Medieval Romances* shows,[15] many early heroic narratives have circulated in the Irish language all through the nineteenth century and up until our own time.

Thus we can see that the archetype of the heroic Finn in the oral tradition can be identified with the characterizations of the hero in the older, more learned traditions. The Irish peasant had no need for an updated Finn remolded in plaster or bronze, like Tennyson's Arthur. But, as Gerard Murphy has pointed out in the introduction to Volume III of *Duanaire Finn,* the unlettered tradition tended to prefer different tales about the hero, tales which stressed a wider range of emotion. To a degree this wider range can be measured by the popularity Finn enjoyed in oral tradition, a popularity which eclipsed traditions surrounding Cúchulainn, a matter which has been the subject of commentary by Douglas Hyde as well as by Gerard Murphy.[16] Perhaps the Ulster Cycle with its "Aristocratic" prevenience, as Yeats liked to say, could hardly be expected to capture the taste of unlettered storytellers. Padraic Colum has suggested that it was Finn's variableness which helped him to replace Cúchulainn in the affections of the Irish peasantry; they saw him as crafty as well as brave, vindictive as well as generous.[17] And, as Gerard Murphy points out in his study, *Ossianic Lore and Tales of Medieval Ireland,* the duplicity in Finn's character is also recorded in manuscript tales, beginning as early as the fifteenth century.[18]

Though the oral-folk Finn may be earthier than the manuscript heroic Finn, it does not mean that he is some kind of Irish Brueghel figure dancing in the Fragonard milieu of the manuscript tradition. Even in the manuscript, Finn was frequently the subject of supernatural practical jokes, as in the series of tales known as *"bruidhean,"* or "magic dwelling" from the conventional first word of their titles. In the *"bruidhean"* tales the hero and his men attempt to attack and take a magic dwelling but in the process become stuck to the chairs and floors, much like Theseus and Pirithous in Hades, so that they cannot be extricated without help, frequently at the expense of portions of their posteriors. Despite this indignity, manuscript authors never try to humiliate the hero or make him look ridiculous, as Vivian Mercier notes with some surprise in *The Irish Comic Tradition*.[19] And, as we have noted earlier, the manuscript authors apparently bowdlerized the stories, attributing to Conan Máol what could not be excised entirely.

Finn's vulnerability to contretemps may have appeared as early as the eighth century in "The Quarrel Between Finn and Oisín," which Kuno Meyer included in his *Fianaigecht*.[20] As the title implies, Finn is at odds with his son in this tale, a perilous role for a father to play. As Vivian Mercier remarks, a son, like Oedipus, who rises against his father is always tragic, but his father, Laius, or any equivalent tends to become comic.[21] But, as Mercier had pointed out earlier in his study,[22] Finn faces defilement and abuse in earlier texts, sometimes at the hand of Oisín, but it was not until later recordings of oral tradition, a project barely begun before, that he is humiliated or made to look ridiculous. Although the literary records do not give us an abused, defiled, and absurd Finn until the nineteenth century, there is reason to believe that the hero was the object of Oedipal attack for many centuries in manuscripts which have not survived, as David Krause has argued in his insightful essay, "The Hidden Oisín."[23] As the object of his son's abuse, Finn must bear many symbolic burdens—authority, paternity, duty, etc.— and in the attack of Oisín sharpens many of his rhetorical tools, some of which he will have to use against the authority of Saint Patrick in the *Acallamh na Senórach* and the ballads built on the same frame. But unlike Cúchulainn, Finn never had to engage in battle with his son; and perhaps for that reason the father's bravery in battle is never called into question. The son may call the father senile, but he never calls him a coward or otherwise challenges his heroism.

Of all the tales about Finn which picture him as an absurd anti-hero, the one in widest circulation in the nineteenth and twentieth centuries is usually known by the title given it by William Carleton, "A Legend of Knockmany," from a hill in Carleton's native County Tyrone. Carleton was a novelist and a storyteller, of course, and not a folklorist, but he sprang from the Gaelic-speaking peasantry and knew volumes of peasant lore, including oral traditions dating to ancient times, more than any other Irish novelist of his century. Indeed, Carleton's authenticity in using materials from peasant life and from oral tradition has made him a source for historians and folklorists. As Carleton's "Knockmany" was written shortly after his conversion to Protestantism and during his association with the fierce anti-papist Caesar Otway, he unquestionably altered his vision of the Gaelic past, as we shall see, but his immediate circumstances could not make him less a peasant.

In Carleton's "Legend of Knockmany," Finn (here spelled "Fin M'Coul") is at work on the Giant's Causeway when he hears that another giant, named Cucullin, spelled without the aspiration in the second syllable, is on his way for a match of strength between them. Let us not be troubled for a moment that Cúchulainn is the hero of another cycle and never appears in any Fenian literature, oral or manuscript, recorded before 1700. Purity had departed Gaelic tradition even before the death of the last of the bards. Finn returns home to his wife, Oonagh, at Knockmany, quaking with fear, sure that he is going to be "skivered like a rabbit" by his enemy. Oonagh is more confident, knowing that the rival giant's power resides in the middle finger of his right hand, and so sets about to outwit him. She has Finn dress as a baby and hide in an unnamed son's cradle, while she prepares to bake bread in which she has inserted granite stones. Giving false hospitality to Cucullin, who is annoyed at not finding Finn home, Oonagh offers Cucullin the granite bread. After failing twice to eat the bread, losing teeth in each attempt, Cucullin refuses to take another bite, at which Oonagh offers another loaf of bread, this one without the granite insert, to Finn, whom she blandly describes as her baby. Finn, of course, has no difficulty at all, which gives Cucullin some amazed apprehension about confronting the father of such a child. Cucullin now wants to leave Knockmany, but not before feeling the teeth of such an astonishing infant. Readying for the climax, Oonagh invites Cucullin to place his magic middle finger well into Finn's mouth. Finn immediately bites the finger off, jumps from the cradle, and makes short work of the rival giant—now debilitated.[24] Our hero has been victorious, but at the price of showing us his cowardice, chicanery, and buffoonery; a hero who has been disguised as a baby by his wife has been made a fool, no matter what a happy purpose it may serve. There are many earlier examples of Finn's guile as a trickster, but in no earlier narrative is he so absurdly anti-heroic.

Carleton's version of this story is but one, the best-known and most widely circulated, as we have said. Yeats, for example, includes it in his *Irish Fairy and Folk Tales*. The next best-known version comes from Patrick Kennedy, the early folktale collector, who published an Anglo-Irish version of what is obviously the same tale in his *Legendary Fictions of the Irish Celts* in 1866.[25] A number of details are changed, e.g., the loaves of bread become griddle cakes, and the rival giant is induced to play a game of fingerstones, but the outcome of the action is the same. The most important change is that the rival giant is not Cúchulainn but rather a Scotsman who wades across the Sea of Moyle on the route of the Giant's Causeway.

The rival giant is also a Scotsman in a version Frederick Marryat puts in the mouth of an Irish character named O'Brien in his *Peter Simple*, first published in 1834.[26] To confuse matters further, Finn is here called "Fingal" and O'Brien must deal with Macpherson's charges that the Fe-

nian tales are Scottish rather than Irish. Also significant is the
reduction of the violence in the tale; the rival runs off as soon
as he sees that Finn can eat the loaves of bread. Finn is less a
fool here because the idea for the infant disguise is his, not
his wife's.

The most interesting version of the narrative is one to be
found in an 1833 issue of the *Dublin Penny Journal*.[27] It is
anonymous, attributed to an author known only as "Q," and,
to my knowledge, has not been the subject of any commentary. Although the tone of the piece suggests an author from
the landlord class, the congruity of detail with other versions
suggests that it, too, is based on a bona-fide folktale. Again,
there are numerous minor variations in detail, such as a
change of location to Ballynascorney near Dublin, but there
is also an exceedingly important one. This time the other
giant comes from Scotland again, but he is Oisín, or
"Ussheen," Finn's own son.

What are we to make of this? Although the *Dublin
Penny Journal* version is contemporary with Carleton's, we
may assume that the inclusion of the Oedipal motif is
enough to assure us that the former is the older, making a
link, as it does, with stories from the eighth century. As
further evidence of Carleton's later composition we cannot
overlook his untraditional substitution of Cúchulainn for a
Fenian name such as Oisín; if the rival giant is indeed Oisín,
then Carleton's substitution would fit with Gerard Murphy's
advice about lettered authors' desire to bowdlerize. And if
the *Dublin Penny Journal* version indeed be closest to the
original, then we have seen the Oedipal attack upon the
hero, an ancient, even primordial theme, linked with the
modern anti-heroic theme. In all the versions of this story we
have called "Knockmany," our sentiments are always with
Finn, and in the end he always prevails, but always at great
expense to his dignity.

The critical question of why Carleton would prefer the

bowdlerized telling of the narrative is unresolved. One safe speculation is that Carleton took on the story to please Caesar Otway's vision of the boorishness of Irish tradition, much as Otway himself had published some comic Fenian stories of his own a few years earlier.[28] Removing the Oedipal motif may simply have made the story more acceptable to the sterner Protestant publishers. Or his substitution may merely have been shrewd; in the nineteenth century the laundered version was bound to be more acceptable to all readers, regardless of class or religion.

The Finn MacCool of "Knockmany" is but one portrayal of an unheroic Finn; there are in addition several others. One which survives from earlier antecedents is the aging, jealous cuckold of the "Pursuit of Diarmuid and Gráinne," a tale which was popular with lettered and unlettered alike; we have on record twenty-six Irish and four Highland oral versions,[29] not to mention modern English-language dramas by Alice Milligan, George Moore and Yeats, Lady Gregory, and Padraic Fallon. This story, too, relies heavily on Oedipal tensions as Gráinne, the beautiful, young betrothed of Finn, has run off with Diarmuid, a favored member of the Fianna and an obvious son-surrogate of the older hero. But Finn, although an abused father and a cuckold, is not in any sense comic in this tale; instead he is vicious and villainous. Late in the tale when Diarmuid has been fatally wounded, Finn stands over his body gloating that all the women of Ireland should see the young hero now—and that they would now no longer admire his beauty. Diarmuid dies when Finn fails to help him. This portrayal is not, as we have suggested, unique to the nineteenth century; several versions of the narrative from six centuries earlier have survived with the significant details intact. The large number of narratives collected from the peasantry during the period of 1800-1916 may only be the result of assiduous collecting rather than a change of attitude; the apparent popularity of the tale may come from its intrinsic merits, to which Finn's portrayal is only incidental. In any case, we are obliged to note that the unfavorable characterization was current, too.

One of the suppositions we have made to justify this excursion into Fenian lore of the nineteenth century is that it would help us to approach the mind of the Irish peasant of 1800-1916. What do we know about that mind? The most obvious discovery is that oral tradition in the Irish language offered the mind of the peasant more sustenance than he would find in mere folklore or märchen, wish-fulfilling stories for entertainment. The Irish oral tradition, robbed of the cultivated leadership it had had in earlier centuries and at lowest ebb aesthetically, contained a mature body of literature which incorporated a wide range of human experience that was distinctly Irish though with universal implications. A peasant sustained on such a tradition does not risk the diminution of identity suffered by his more affluent brothers who have been homogenized in foreign lands, or even in the commercial capital of Dublin.

And what of the divided vision the Irish peasant has of his national hero, Finn MacCool? The short answer to that question was given by Standish James O'Grady in 1878 when he remarked in his legendary *History of Ireland* that "Heroes expand into giants, and dwindle into goblins, or fling aside the heroic form and gambol as buffoons. . . ."[30] Aside from anticipating a number of anthropological theorists of the next generation, O'Grady is telling us more. Because Irish tradition was still alive in oral tradition, the peasant can choose from the tradition which best suits him. If the peasant sees himself as a beaten man in his own country, his culture offers him two visions. He can remember the hyperbolic heroic tradition of the past and arm himself for a struggle greater than he may be able to accomplish. Or if this is too terrifying, the Fenian literature offers an alternative.

Like the Czechs at the other edge of the Germanic world who in modern times made a national hero of the Good Soldier Schweik, the Irish could see that stealth and guile, not to mention silence and cunning, were useful to a people who lacked the physical and financial power to overcome visiting giants sure to win in a test of strength. There may be nothing heroic in the silence and cunning of the unlettered peasant, but they are preferable to exile.

[1]The proper Irish spelling of the name is, of course, Fionn mac Cumhaill; I have used the standardized English form as I find it preferred by a majority of disinterested scholars and by most contemporary Irishmen.

[2]*Transactions of the Ossianic Society*, 3 (1857), p. 28.

[3]*Popular Tales of the West-Highlands*, Orally Collected (Paisley: Gardner, 1861), I, xiii.

[4]Myles Dillon, *Cycles of Kings* (Oxford: Oxford University Press, 1946).

[5]John V. Kelleher, "Ossian and the Irish," an address given to the American Committee for Irish Studies, University of Michigan, Ann Arbor, May 3, 1973.

[6]D. K. Wilgus, from roundtable discussion following the reading of this paper in Oneonta, New York, April 7, 1973.

[7]*Duanaire Finn*, III, Irish Texts Society, No. 43 (Dublin: Educational Company of Ireland, 1953), pp. xxxvii-xl.

[8]*Duanaire Finn*, III, pp. xxiv-xxix. In the discussion following the reading of this paper, Professor E. Estyn Evans remarked that oral tradition is now more in line with manuscript; in 1969 he met a farmer in County Cavan who told him that Finn was not really a giant at all: "He's only 5'6"," the man said.

[9]*Duanaire Finn*, III, pp. xl, xlii-xliii, xcix, and 188-189.

[10]See D. K. Wilgus, "Irish Traditional Narrative Songs in English: 1800-1916," included in this collection of essays.

[11]The *Kiltartan Poetry* (1919), *History* (1909), and *Wonder Books* (1910) have recently been reissued in one volume (Garrards Cross: Colin Smythe; New York: Oxford University Press, 1971).

[12]Gregory, *Kiltartan History Book*, pp. 70-71.

[13]T. D. MacDonald, *Gaelic Proverbs and Proverbial Sayings* (Stirling: Eneas Mackay, 1926), pp. 133-139.

[14]MacDonald, pp. 137,136.

[15]Bruford, *Gaelic Folktales and Medieval Romances* (Dublin: Folklore of Ireland Society, 1969), pp. 250-267.

[16]Hyde, *A Literary History of Ireland* (London: T. Fisher, Unwin, 1899), pp. 374-375, *et passim*. Cf. *Duanaire Finn*, III, pp. iii, xiii.

[17]*The Frenzied Prince* (Philadelphia: McKay, 1943), p. 194.

[18]Murphy, *Ossianic Lore and Tales of Medieval Ireland* (Dublin: At the Three Candles, 1961), pp. 30-31.

[19]*Irish Comic Tradition* (New York: Oxford University Press, 1962), p. 20.

[20]*Fianaigecht, Being a Collection of Hitherto Unedited Irish Poems and Tales Relating to Finn and His Fiana,* . . . Royal Irish Academy, Todd Lecture Series, Vol. 16 (Dublin: Hodges, Figgis; London: Williams and Norgate, 1910), pp. 22-23.

[21]Mercier, p. 32.

[22]Mercier, p. 20.

[23]Krause, "The Hidden Oisín," *Studia Hibernica*, 6 (1966), pp. 7-24.

[24]"A Legend of Knockmany" was originally published in *Traits and Stories of the Irish Peasantry, 1830-1833*, volumes quite rare today; the text used for this summary is *Tales and Sketches, Illustrating the Character, Usages, Traditions, Spirits, and Pastimes of the Irish Peasantry* (Dublin: J. Duffy, 1845), pp. 97-112.

[25](London: Macmillan, 1866), pp. 203-205.

[26]Although *Peter Simple* was first published in London by Bentley in 1834, the text I have used is Volume 9 of the *Collected Novels* (Boston: Colonial Press, 1897), pp. 90-92. The episode is in chapter 12 of the novel.

[27]"A Legend of Fin Mac-Cool," *DPJ*, 1, #41 (April 6, 1833), pp. 327-328.

[28]"Salmon of Finn MacCool" *Sketches in Ireland*, etc. (Dublin: W. Curry, 1827), pp. 129-200.

[29]Nessa Ni Sheaghdha, ed., *Tóraigheacht Dhiarmada agus Ghráinne*, Irish Text Society, Vol. 48 (Dublin: Educational Company of Ireland, 1967), pp. xviii-xix; cf. Alan Bruford, pp. 106-109, pp. 265-366.

[30](Dublin: Ponsonby, 1878), p. 28.

D . K . W I L G U S

# Irish Traditional Narrative
# Songs in English: 1800-1916

THOUGH THE COMPLICATED process of indexing and cataloguing Irish traditional narrative songs begins with this study,
there are a number of valuable insights into native Irish
traditions and into the songs of the Irish peasantry that
emerge for both musicologist and folklorist.[1] Naturally the
study suffers from the limitations of initial explorations in
that it elicits preliminary data that contribute as much to the
methodology for indexing and cataloguing and to the appre-
ciation of the comparative English-language folksong tradition as it does to an understanding of historical and socio-

D. K. Wilgus is Professor of English and Anglo-American Folksong and
Chairman of the Folklore and Mythology Group at University of California, Los Angeles. He has been a president of the American Folklore
Society and has authored and edited three volumes on folksong and
folklore, as well as numerous articles and sound recordings.

The research on which this study is based has been supported by
grants from the Ford Foundation, the American Council of Learned
Societies, the American Philosophical Society, and the Humanities Institute, the Research Committee of the Academic Senate, and the Center
for the Study of Comparative Folklore and Mythology, University of
California, Los Angeles. Materials from the Irish Folklore Collections,
Irish Folklore Department, University College, Dublin, are quoted by
permission of Bo Almqvist, chairman. Great thanks are owed Professor
Seán Ó Súlleabháin for his aid in enlightenment in areas in which the
author was quite ignorant, and to Thomas Munnelly, who was both Irish
research assistant and friend and companion in much of the author's work
in Ireland.

logical dimensions of the Irish peasant in the 1800-1916 period.[2]

In terms of the large corpus of materials available, we cannot even survey here the problems of themes and styles. Where to begin? Matters of form and style, themes and subject matter are so closely related in the situation of cultural contact followed by the dominance—or apparent dominance—of one of the cultures that separation is difficult. If one begins with the bilingual situation which existed in varying degrees in different areas during the nineteenth century, one finds considerable scattered comment on the problem throughout the literature, but—to my knowledge—no incisive treatment. A recent report by Hugh Shields of his song collecting in a bilingual parish in Donegal[3] indicates what study should have been done previously. But surviving texts do give us some information as to the situation in the nineteenth century. (I emphasize that I am, of necessity, avoiding as far as possible important areas of musical tradition, performance style, etc.)

In the surviving materials we find a relatively small but significant number of narrative song texts indicating a varied relationship between the Gaelic and Irish linguistic tradition in individual songs. Some few English ballads occur in translated Gaelic versions, and some few Gaelic narrative songs move into the English-language tradition. The most direct and consequently the most puzzling tradition is that of what seems to have been an original Gaelic song which has moved into English-language tradition, in which it appears in varying forms. The Irish texts of *Fáinne Gael an Lae,* "The Dawning of the Day," seem to precede the English, though English songs like "Rolling in the Dew Makes the Mild Maid Fair" might raise a question as to the basic tradition. The narrative begins with an encounter of a young man and a maid, with various results: there may be a simple conversation; she may refuse to stay with him; he may seek to marry her and be rejected; they may agree to marry and do so; he may seduce her and later refuse to marry her. It will be useful at this point to outline four narrative types and the textual differences.

I. Unsuccessful Courtship

A. A macaronic form, largely interstanzaic repetitive; that is, a stanza in Gaelic is followed by a stanza in English translation. The one text in this form, however, is not consistent. The first English stanza:

> One morning fair as I roved out
> All in the summer time,
> Each bush and tree was dressed in green,
> And valleys in their prime.
> As on by bower and town and tower
> And widespread fields I strayed.
> I met a maid in the greenwood shade
> By the dawning of the day.

B. The 1847 "literary" translation by Edward Walsh, which has been reported from oral tradition:

> At early dawn I once had been
> Where Lene's blue waters flow,
> When summer bid the groves be green,
> The lamp of light to glow,
> As on by bow'r and town and tow'r
> And widespread fields I stray,
> I met a maid in the green-wood shade
> At the dawning of the day.

C. P. W. Joyce's translation of 1873, not reported from traditional sources:

> One morning early I walked forth

By the margin of Lough Lene;
The sunshine dressed the trees in green,
And summer bloomed again;
I left the town and wandered on
Through fields all green and gay,
And who should I meet but Cooleen Dhas,
By the dawning of the day.

D. A translation credited to N. Clifford, not reported
from oral tradition. It seems a slight variation of that
by Joyce:

One morning early as I walked out by the margin of
Lough Leine.
The sun shines across the trees in green,
the Summer blooms again,
I left the town and wandered down the fields
all green and gay.
I met a maid, a comely maid, at the Dawning
of the day.

E. Broadside text with no indication of source:

As I walked forth one morning before the
break of day,
Across the pleasant field so gay I carelessly
did stray;
I there espied a comely lass, she seemed the
Queen of May,
As she lightly tripped o'er the meadows green
At the dawning of the day.

II. Greeting but not courtship. (This is a "fragment" of
Type III, but it must be treated as a distinct type in its
establishment of a single narrative unit.)

III.  Seduction and Rejection:

> As I roved out one morning, it being in the
>     summer time,
> Each bush and tree were decked with green and
>     the valleys in their prime.
> In returning home all from a wake through
>     the field I took my way.
> It was there I spied a comely maid by the
>     dawning of the day.

IV.  Successful Courtship.

A.  She agrees to marry him the next time he comes that
    way, and they are finally married:

> As the sun rose high in the morning sky
>     and the fields were wet with dew,
> I strayed beside the Bandon's side where
>     the woodbine sweetly grew.
> I heard a song in the woods along like the
>     thrush's morning lay.
> It was a comely maid who quietly strayed
>     at the dawning of the day.

B.  After winning her love, he gives her a ring before he
    leaves. He returns in six months and makes her his
    wife.

> Returning home from a wake one night
> It was through the field I chanced to stray.
> It was there I spied an angel so charming and
>     so gay
> And she going to milk her cows by the dawning
>     of the day.[4]

The four narrative types seem to represent at least seven independent translations. As our sampling may represent only the tip of the iceberg, we are left to wonder how much the English-language tradition owes to independent translation from the Gaelic and how much to variation within the English-language tradition. Full study of more evidence is obviously required.

Macaronic or bilingual songs, as we have them, show a great deal of variety. They may be interstanzaic or inter- linear; the Gaelic and English may repeat each other, or the song may continue in the two languages so that one must be bilingual to understand the song. The songs sometimes exist in Gaelic, macaronic, and English versions. And in some cases the Gaelic and English are mixed in various ways. Some macaronic ballads appear on broadsides, and it seems a toss-up which is more "corrupt," the English or the Gaelic. In most cases I posit a Gaelic original, which is clear in such a macaronic as "Baile An Láoi," a bilingual form of "Mary Hynes" or "The Posy Bright," attributed to the turn-of-the- nineteenth-century bard Anthony Raftery.[5] However, the Anglo "Soldier, Won't You Marry Me?" occurs in both macaronic and fully Gaelic versions.[6] There are cases, how- ever, in which the bilingual form seems original. In the dialogue song "The *Seoinín's* Proposal" the girl will speak only Gaelic in reply to the *seoinín* (one following English fashion) who, speaking only English, proposes marriage and offers her a life "among our tony set" and possibly a life in London. She refuses him, preferring a poor Gaelic man and to die in Ireland.[7] That there were considerably more of these bilingual texts than the more than fifty I have noted is open to question; but their survival into the middle of the twentieth century supports such a conjecture.

Before we look further into the corpus or repertoire, we might raise briefly the problem of authorship of the songs. Because I am considering all narrative songs found in oral

tradition, some of the material comes from music hall tradition and other sources at some remove from the folk. On the
other hand, there is considerable evidence that much of the
material originated on the folk level. This seems to be true of
a good deal of the material traceable to broadsides. Granted
that students like Oliver Goldsmith (like the young Ben-
jamin Franklin in North America) contributed to the penny
press, the ballad printers were the repositories and distribu-
tors of considerable material originated on another level.
Ballad printers are almost invariably ballad collectors, and
in some instances the ballad composers and hawkers en-
gaged printers to issue their wares instead of simply taking
others from stock. Skellig lists are cases in point.

In the southwest of Ireland it was customary to compose and circulate on Shrove Tuesday rhyming catalogues
of unmarried men and women who were to undertake a
supposed pilgrimage to the Skelligs rocks. (These are mainly satirical catalogues, but those few involving fictitious
narrative come within my purview.) Thomas Crofton
Croker reported that in the 1830s Cork printers issued thousands of them on the commission of their composers.[8] The
extent to which the unnamed composers are to be considered "folk"—though this was clearly a traditional custom—
could perhaps be argued. And attributions of authorship—
Croker usually suggests somewhat cultivated sources—are
always open to question. But many known poets of nineteenth-century Ireland, whatever their cultivation, were of
necessity close to the folk. Patrick O'Kelly, the author of
"The Doneraile Litany," cursed the town where he lost his
watch.[9] There is one report of the rhymed curse from
twentieth-century tradition,[10] and it seems to have inspired
"The Curse of Beeing," in which a bard curses the village
where his buggy whip is stolen.[11]

The bards of Ireland, forced by circumstance onto a
"folk" level, certainly maintained a traditional status in the

nineteenth century, for in the twentieth century the belief in
their power over rats persisted.[12] Whether by music or other
means, the poets could banish or sometimes summon the
rodents. One of my favorite accounts is of the poet who

> went into the house one night and the people of the
> house were tormented with a big rat. The poet got a sod
> of turf and put it in the middle of the floor. Then he put
> a razor on top of it and said some words. Soon the rat
> was heard coming and he was roaring. Then he lay
> down near the sod and cut his throat with the razor.[13]

There is indeed a ballad beginning

> It is spacious, clean, inviting and
> Beside the Ruagach stream doth stand
> And once upon a time a plague
> Of rats infested Drimolague

which tells how a "bardie son of Drimolague" charms the
rats and marches them to Ross, where the tide bears them
off to sea. The poet is identified as "one O'Sullivan, then
Bard and Genius of Drimolague."[14]

Of course traditional attributions of authorship to local
poets must always be examined carefully and sometimes
seen as more traditional than accurate. For example, a
rhyme composed by the bard after hearing Thomas Moore's
"Vale of Avoca" is attached to a number of local poets, this
version to "George Curtin" (Mike Twomey) of County
Cork:

> Sweet Vale of Avoca, though Tom Moore called
> you sweet,
> If he had to walk on the road without shoes
> on his feet,

Or lie on a bed without blanket or sheet,
He wouldn't give a damn where the bright
    waters meet.[15]

Yet "Curtin" certainly did compose some of the songs
attributed to him, such as "Matt Twomey's Cottage" and
two songs called "The Man Who Came Home from Pretoria."[16] One would reject the attribution of "Red River
Valley" to Francis Travers of County Monaghan,[17] but the
celebrated Cornelius Ahearne of County Cork could have
composed "The Groves of Dripsy,"[18] "Bonnie Young Katie
from Sweet Donoughmore,"[19] and "The Maid of Mill-
street,"[20] if not "The Can of Spring Water."[21] Like Raftery,
his death was celebrated in traditional song.[22] Attributions
can be validated only by intense study, if then. But local
poets, wandering bards, and hedge schoolmasters certainly
had a great share in the launching of nineteenth-century
traditional song.

In surveying the subject matter of the traditional narrative songs in the nineteenth century, I want to avoid any
dreary parade of statistics to demonstrate range and popularity. Rather I want to concentrate on what seems to be
typical and distinctive in the subject matter and style of the
narratives. Irish singers originated and preserved narratives
encompassing the usual range of Anglo-American subjects,
with especial emphases in theme and style. Many songs are
in typical vulgar ballad style, with the well-known journalistic approach. A considerable number adopt a more senti-
mental or pastoral tone consistent with the Irish stereotype.
But one may be surprised at the small number of narratives
in English dealing with fairies, ghosts, and the Christian
religion, although there are a number of songs in the religio-
political field. Indeed, the outstanding Christian reference is
the modification of the "Come-all-ye" opening commonplace to "Come all ye feeling-hearted Christians" or
"Come all ye Roman Catholics."

Although historical songs bulk small in the general Anglo-American repertoire, they form a considerable portion of the Irish narratives, for reasons not hard to seek. The troubled history of Ireland furnishes a direct source for song and accounts especially for the persistence of large numbers of songs of protest or rebellion, which were of less incidence in other Anglo-American areas and did not persist long in tradition. Then, too, the necessity of many Irish youths enlisting in the English army and navy to serve on foreign soil gave a special flavor to love and separation. Even the emigration songs have an historical cast.

I should devote considerable discussion to songs dealing with the political and social struggles. However, Georges-Denis Zimmermann has surveyed this field recently in his *Songs of Irish Rebellion* (Hatboro, Pennsylvania, 1967). It should be noted, however, that Zimmermann's sources are predominately broadsides. Certainly the majority of the songs were in oral tradition, and more than half of them survived into the twentieth century. But because of dependence on broadsides and because of problems of space, some dimensions are lacking. Only when one looks at the songs surviving into the twentieth century does one realize the extent to which political and social events were the subject of the ballad muse. It seems as if every eviction, every boycott, every assassination or attempted assassination called forth an appropriate ballad or ballads. And, of course, ballads that would be classified under "criminal" rubrics often belong to social and political history. Was it a crime for an Irish peasant to shoot an English land agent or for a Protestant group to massacre members of a Papist parade? One example is the group of ballads clustering around William Sydney Clements, third Earl of Leitrim. (He is often confused in tradition with the older brother Robert or his nephew Robert, fourth Earl.) He is remembered, among other things for harsh and eccentric treatment of tenants and for his alleged exercise of *le droit de seigneur*. There is a ballad of his attempt to "knock" Gortelattragh Chapel in 1856, but most of the song material is related to his assassination in Donegal, April 2, 1878. (The assassin in the ballads is the traditional "Rory of the Hill.") There seem to be at least nine ballads and a lyric celebration dealing with his death. The death of one of his alleged assassins in Lifford Jail (though tradition says he was smuggled out alive) was the subject of another ballad, and Lord Leitrim's name crops up in other later songs. And there is a song purportedly by one of the assassins lamenting his exile.[23] I was still able to collect songs and traditions in Leitrim in 1969, and I suspect they still flourish in Donegal, where there is a monument to the three assassins.

A good deal has been written concerning the *aisling* or vision song, one form of which occurs as a political allegory in which the girl who appears as a symbol of Ireland weeping for national subjection or the death of a leader.[24] Narrative songs in English in this pattern are attached to most of the crucial political events of nineteenth-century Ireland, and associated with Napoleon, Robert Emmett, Michael Davitt, Daniel O'Connell, Charles Parnell, John Dillon, and others. (I have not found all the aislingi in tradition.) There is considerable dispute concerning the relationship of the allegorical-aisling to the love-aisling and prophecy-aisling of earlier Gaelic tradition. All English language allegorical-aislingi do not employ a female figure, witness the mid-19th-century "Rights of Man," which is now employed by the Civil Rights Movement in the Six Counties.[25] But there is certainly, in the tradition of Irish political song, the habit of turning other kinds of songs into political allegories, as for example the pattern of fox-hunting song is used to tell the story of Michael Hayes, on the run for shooting a land agent in the 1960s.[26] So it is not surprising that in the English-language tradition the allegorical-aisling

blends into the love-aisling and into the pastourelle (which
may also be used politically). Often the difference between
the genres is apparent only after the girl identifies herself.
"The Cailin Deas" ("The Nice Girl") begins:

> One evening fair for to take the air as the
>     summer sun went down,
> The moon all her beauties rare the stars began
>     to crown,
> By Dublin's Bay I chanced to stray where a female
>     form did pass.
> More brighter by far than the evening star, and
>     they call her the Cailin Deas.

The narrator asks her name and dwelling. She tells him she is
the daughter of Brian the Brave and likes to roam by the
plain where he died. He closes his eyes and departs.[27]
"Bonny Young Katie from Sweet Donoughmore" begins:

> As I went walking one morning so early
> And steered my course eastwards towards
>     Donoughmore fair,
> To worship old Bacchus and court the acquaintance
> Of some of the fair maids most beautiful there.
> Whilst thus contemplating the goodness of Nature,
> The fields there with daisies were scattered all o'er,
> My fortune I there met, that blooming fair one
> Called Bonny Young Katie from sweet Donough-
>     more.[28]

Some songs that begin thus will close after the effusive
pseudo-literary description, in which case I must treat the
song as a lyric and exclude it from the catalogue. This song,
however, continues in hedge schoolmaster-fashion with
what we may call "the goddess routine." He addresses her,

asking if she is one of a number of goddesses of classical mythology. She denies the imputation. He declares his love, after which they go to the fair and have a great day drinking and dancing among her relations.

From the point in such a song at which she denies being a goddess, sometimes berating him for his flattery, the narrative can branch into almost any conceivable plot variation: rejection, seduction, desertion, marriage, etc. The disputation is often conducted in such pseudo-elegant language and at such length that an American field worker might doubt that such a song as "The Phoenix of the Hall" was ever a part of folk tradition.

> One day for recreation in silent meditation near
> a sweet plantation I carelessly did stray,
> Where Flora's decoration enriched each situation,
> a rural habitation that lay along the way.
> Being wrapt in contemplation and viewing the
> creation,
> I thought for to extol,
> When to my admiration I saw a constellation whose
> proper appellation was the Phoenix of the Hall.

He courts her, she initially rejects him, but in some versions the narrative continues with an acceptance.[29] Even longer is "The True Lover's Discussion."

> One pleasant evening as pinks and daisies
> Closed in their bosoms a drop of dew,
> The feathered warblers of every species
> Together changed their notes so true,
> As I did stray, wrapped in meditation,
> It charmed my heart to hear them sing.
> The silent orbs of night were just arising,
> And the air in concert did sweetly sing.

This song has more of a *chanson d'aventure* pattern, as the narrator observes the disputation of two lovers. The lass tells the lad that she is rejecting him for a youth of birth and fortune and that her parents would be offended were she to choose him. There is a long dialogue in which he denounces her as a deceiver and she advances the fickleness of men. He denounces her and bids her farewell. Some versions continue with the maid proclaiming that she was only testing him, asking his forgiveness, and threatening to remain single if he will not marry her; other versions have little more than the long metaphorical debate.[30] Not only is this song well attested in reports from tradition, but I heard it from a Donegal singer in 1969.

Such debates sometimes occur in a religious vein, with the couple arguing the sectarian beliefs which divide them. Rarely, as in "The Lady's Conversion to Catholicity,"[31] the "heretic" is female; more often, e.g., "Charming Townley Hall"[32] and "Pride of Dundalk (Sligo) Town,"[33] the male is converted to "the holy church of Rome." "The Banks of Dunmore" opens:

> You lovers of high and low station and gentlemen
>     all of renown,
> Give ear unto those few verses I lately have penned
>     down
> In praise of a fair maiden that lately from my bosom
>     my heart has torn,
> And she's but a poor farmer's daughter that lives
>     on the banks of Dunmore.

The narrator addresses her, tells her of his wealth, and offers to make her his equal. She replies that they are "not of one persuasion," as she is Catholic and cannot marry him unless he is converted. He challenges her to refute his religion by Scripture, which she does. He agrees to embrace Catholicism and they are married.[34]

Certain of the preceding examples illustrate another stylistic characteristic of many songs in the English-language tradition: the conscious or unconscious attempt to imitate in English the assonantal patterns of Gaelic poetry. Too often the assonance turns into complicated infelicitous rhyme, though it apparently accorded with the folk esthetic:

> Ye brilliant muses who ne'er refuses but still
>   confuses on the poet's mind,
> Your strong sweet favor to my endeavor, if my
>   ardent favors appear sublime,
> Protect my study from getting muddy by ideas
>   read to inspire my brain,
> And my quill refine while I write these lines on
>   a simple divine called the Star of Slane.[35]

I grant that internal rhyme is a feature of much English blackletter broadside poetry, but I think the ancestry of that needs looking into as well.

Songs of courtship are far more numerous and varied than I have indicated, though the types mentioned are among the most distinctively Irish. Ballad plots involve parental disapproval, death, return in disguise, female warriors, etc.—a rather rich budget of themes generally known in Anglo-American balladry, yet often with distinctive Irish flavor.

We find both the flavor and emphasis in other areas. While disaster ballads are an Anglo-American staple and we can note a ballad of "The Big Wind" of 1839[36] and four ballads of "The Moving Bog,"[37] we can find in some tragedy ballads distinct patterns and emphases. "The Lakes of Cool Finn" (Laws Q 33) was once tentatively interpreted to have some sort of supernatural theme, but comparision with ballads such as "Noble Tom Campbell,"[38] "The Drowning of John Cullen,"[39] "James Judge,"[40] "Denny Murphy,"[41] and

"Sloan Wellesley"[42] reveals "simply" but distinctly a song pattern of drowning in local loughs. However, "The Wreck of the Ferry Boat" tells how a wife disregards her husband's premonition of danger from fairies and sets out across the river on a boat which is destroyed by the agency of the fairies Simon Hanly, Simon Tonry, and Dun Bingham.[43]

The number of ballads of boat wrecks and ship wrecks is not surprising, given local conditions—insular Ireland, the fishing industry, the trips of laborers to the Scottish harvests, the percentage of Irish on merchant ships, the large number of emigrants, particularly in the "coffin ships" of the Famine period, and the shipbuilding industry itself. I should mention at this point the ballads of the sinking of the *Titanic*, in which I have a special interest. As ballads of the disaster are known in a number of languages and the ship had an Irish birth, it is not surprising that there were seven Irish ballads on the 1912 tragedy, nor that I was able to record one in 1969.[44] But if not surprising, it is at least interesting that only one of the Irish ballads has anything but praise for the actions of the captain and crew.

Ballads in the broad area of "occupation and experience" are many and diverse. Somewhat surprising are the relatively small number of ballads dealing with farm labor. It must be borne in mind, however, that such a category includes songs not fitting anywhere else and is largely restricted to narratives of poor conditions of hired laborers. Yet there are more songs about farm animals than about working conditions, which makes a significant point about the Irish folk muse. And of course the dearth of industrial ballads is not surprising; those that exist mainly deal with tragedies, again a normal condition.

We can pass over such "standard" subjects as crime and murders; not that these themes were not well represented in nineteenth-century Ireland, but the Irish ballads fit well into the Anglo-American pattern. Two subject-matter areas are,

however, worthy of note. Sporting events are celebrated in
ballads of other Anglo-American areas, but nowhere, I
believe, as frequently as in Ireland. There are narratives of
hunts, horse races, dog races, boat races, boxing, football,
hurling, etc. Some of these, such as "The Kilruddy Hunt,"[45]
stem from sources not particularly peasant or folk, but many
seem to bear the mark of the local, rural bard. Even the
fairies play football:

> As I was going to Annagasson, by chance I met the
>     fairy train.
> They had as fine a football play as e'er was held
>     upon a plain.
> There were thousands from Ardbrasson and bonnet
>     men
>     from Aberdeen;
> They put me out of my latitude, for such a sight
>     I never seen.
> As I was going past the windmills, there came four
>     and twenty meeting me.
> They were loose to the waist and the ball was with
>     them most gallantly.
> I made a few bold dashes at the stoutest hero in
>     my view,
> But soon I was upsetted by a red-haired boy who
>     ran at me.
> I arose in a great fury, to make havoc on the train,
> But I was raised with foot and shoulder by a red-
>     haired boy who ran at me.[46]

The other category is the broad one of humor. Of
course one can find humor in ballads in many subject-matter
areas, e.g. courtship. And it is part of my point that this is
especially true of Irish traditional narrative song. But I am
thinking of a particular type of zany humor that turns up in

songs of parties, wakes, weddings, journeys, animals which behave like humans (often in songs of political or local satire). These songs offend many critics because they smack of the stereotype of the stage Irishman. Indeed, many of them did get a music hall start or circulation. But behind a stereotype lies a truth being caricatured. And certainly the Irish folk have composed, accepted, adopted, and adapted these songs. No "ballad history" or Ireland can ignore them or fail to come to grips with the aspects of Irish life they represent. Analysis of this material will tell us as much about Irish life as any devoted to the more "serious" muse.

I must confess the sketchy and inadequate nature of this survey, which may, however, have indicated the large amount of material involved and the difficulty in coming to grips with it. I hope that when my "tool" is completed, adequate assessment and study will be possible. Such study may seriously alter the few conclusions I have been able to reach. Certainly further comparison between the Gaelic- and English- language traditions will be fruitful.

If I have learned anything from this attempt to assess the ballad materials I am cataloging, it is that I am still underestimating the richness and diversity of Irish folksong. On the basis of the catalogue in its present state, I think I could answer many specific questions related to nineteenth-century Anglo-Irish ballads, but the questions are too many to pose. I am not one who believes that the ballads of an area or period will give us a complete picture or reflection of its political, social, and economic history. But I feel that, if to the narrative songs, we added the remainder of the folksong tradition, the reflection of nineteenth-century Ireland would be more complete than that of any other area or period I know of. Both events and attitudes are represented in some detail. And, if what little I know of Irish history did not all come from the songs, the songs certainly led me to that knowledge.

[1]This extensive work in Irish folksong has been a by-product of a much larger project, a type-index of Anglo-American folk balladry, which is in turn a part of a pan-European type-index being constructed under the aegis of the Deutschen Volksliedarchiv in Freiburg. Cf., *Arbeitstagung uber Fragen des Typenindex der europaischen Volksballaden vom 28.-30. Sept. 1966 in Deutschen Volksliedarchiv in Freiburg i. Breisgau* (Berlin, 1966); *2. Arbeitstagung . . . vom 10 bis 12 April 1969 im Universitatshaus von Cikhaj bei Brno/CSSR* (Berlin, 1969); *3. Arbeitstagung . . . vom 21. bis 23. August 1970 im Kloster Utstein bei Stavanger/Norwegen* (Berlin, 1970); *4. Arbeitstagung . . . vom 21. bis 23. August 1971 im Musee des Arts et Traditions Populaires in Paris* (Berlin, 1971); *5. Arbeitstagung.. . vom 20. bis 24 August 1972 un Skofja Loka, Jugoslawien* (Freiburg, 1973). See also D. K. Wilgus, "A Type-Index of Anglo-American Narrative Songs," *Journal of the Folklore Institute* 7 (1970), 161-76.

The serious collecting of Irish folk music began with Edward Bunting in the last years of the 18th century: *The Ancient Music of Ireland* (Dublin, 1809). He was followed by, among others, Henry Judson, George Petrie, William Forde, John Edward Pigot, James Goodman, and Patrick Weston Joyce. I would not in one whit detract from their importance, but I must point out the limitations of their work for present purposes. The orientation of these collectors was toward the tunes and toward Gaelic texts. Other than references by a few contributors to journals and fugitive publications, serious note of Anglo-Irish folksongs was taken by Patrick Weston Joyce in *Ancient Irish Music* (Dublin, 1873), *Irish Peasant Songs in the English Language* (Dublin, 1903), and *Old Irish Music and Songs* (Dublin, 1909).

[2]Qualifications of my statements about dating comes from the basic problem of discussing the narrative folksongs of a given area at a given period, in this case Ireland, 1800-1916. The songs of this period, for my purpose, are those sung then, not simply those originating during that time. My concept of narrative song, I should point out, is far wider than most definitions of the ballad, wide enough that a large amount of folksong is included.

[3] "Singing Traditions of a Bilingual Parish in North-West Ireland," *Yearbook of the International Folk Music Council*, 3 (1971, issued 1972): 109-19.

[4]References to texts: The Irish Folklore Collections in the Irish Folklore Department, University College, Dublin (formerly the Irish Folklore Commission), will henceforth be referred to as IFC, followed by the *Ms.* volume cited. An "S" prefix before a volume number indicates the *MSS. na Scol* collection.

I. A. *Ireland's Own*, 5 May 1934, p. 577 (Kerry, 1934?).

I. B. Walsh, *Irish Popular Songs* (1847); Samuel Lover, *Lyrics of Ireland* (London, 1858), 325-6; Lover, *Poems of Ireland* (London, 1858), 325-6; *Poetry and Legendary Ballads of the South of Ireland* (Cork, 1894), 155-6;

*Sing an Irish Song* (Dublin, n.d.), Book II; *Universal Irish Song Book* (New York, 1897), 52; *Ireland's Own*, 22 Sept. 1951, p. 13; 27 June 1953, p. 14; James N. Healy, *The Second Book of Irish Ballads* (3d ed., Cork, 1968), 120-1; IFC: S396, pp. 281-2 (Cork, c. 1938); S457 pp. 752-3 (Kerry, ca. 1938); 249, pp. 491-2 (Mayo, 1936).

I. C. Joyce, *Ancient Irish Music* (Dublin, 1873), 8-10; *Irish Music and Song* (London, 1903), 29-30.

I. D. *Ireland's Own*, 22 Sept. 1951, p. 13; 10 Mar. 1956, p. 11; *Songs and Recitations of Ireland*, Book 5 (Cork, 1967), 24.

I. E. *Ireland's Own*, 30 Aug. 1958, p. 11; 12 Nov. 1960, p. 11; *Songs and Recitations of Ireland*, Book 3 (Cork, 1967), 13.

II. IFC: S1125, pp. 25-6 (Cork, 1939).

III. Laws P 16; IFC 287, pp. 157-9 (Mayo, 1936); 782, pp. 38-40 (Kerry, 1941); broadside, National Library; Royal Irish Academy, Dublin, 66.H.17; 12.B1.12; Trinity College, Dublin, 22.0.11.

IV.A. IFC: S326, pp. 215-6 (Cork, ca. 1938); S344, pp. 182-3 (Cork, ca. 1938).

IV.B. IFC: 210-pp. 490-2 (Mayo, 1936).

[5]The macaronic form (Mayo, 1958) is in IFC: Tape 43B (copy in UCLA T7-69-54). For the Gaelic form, see Douglas Hyde, *Ábrain ata leagtha ar an Reachtuire (Songs Ascribed to Raftery)* (Dublin, 1903), 330-35.

[6]The macronic form is in IFC: pp. 371-72 (sent from London, 1957). Francis O'Neill refers to his parents' singing of *"Cailin beag mo Chroidhe"* in *Irish Folk Music: A Fascinating Hobby*, 68. English language forms: IFC:1281, pp. 142-3 (Galway, 1943) Slo96, pp. 127-30 (Galway, 1947), disc 356 (1947); disc 363 (1947); BBC 12489 (Galway, 1947; copies in IFC: disc 901; and UCLA T7-69-49).

[7]IFC: S114, pp. 252-55 (Mayo, ca. 1938).

[8]Thomas Crofton Croker, *Popular Songs of Ireland* (London: 1886), 122-5.

[9]Croker (1886), 176-82.

[10]IFC: S367, pp. 335-8 (Cork, ca. 1938). The text in James N. Healy, *Ballads from the Pubs of Ireland* (Cork, 1965), 44-7, is certainly from a printed source.

[11]IFC: S346, pp. 1602 (Cork, 1938); 1592, p. 144 (Cork, 1960). Authorship is attributed to John Honohan, Donoughmore, Co. Cork.

[12]See Fred Norris Robinson, "Satirists and Enchanters in Early Irish Literature," *Studies in the History of Religions Presented to Crawford Howell Toy* (New York, 1912), 95-130; Bo Almqvist, *Norron Niddiktning: Traditionshistoriska Studier i Versmagi*, 1 (Norron, Goteborg, Uppsala, 1965).

[13]IFC: S356, pp. 132-3. There are countless other references in the IFC *Mss.* to the power of the poets.

[14]IFC: S301, pp. 241-2 (Cork, 1938).

[15]IFC: 1692, p. 457 (Cork, 1961); a variant in ibid., pp. 108 (Cork, 1960.

[16]IFC 737, pp. 161-5 (Cork, 1941); IFC 1591, pp. 220-7, 248-9, 256 (Cork, 1960). There is a third song titled "The Man Who Came Home from Pretoria" (IFC: 1501, pp. 414-5 [sent from England in 1957]), which was more likely "Curtin's" inspiration than his composition.)

[17]IFC: S948 (ca. 1938).

[18]The MacDonagh Collection is part of the IFC and will be referred to as IFC: MacDonagh. IFC: MacDonagh; 1951, pp. 335-50; S325, pp. 59, 190-93; S341, pp. 36-7.

[19]IFC: MacDonagh; 1591, pp. 504-7.

[20]IFC: MacDonagh; 1591, pp. 208-10; S325, p. 54.

[21]IFC: MacDonagh; S325, p. 59; S326, p. 56: W.H. Gratton Flood, *Ireland's Own Song Book* (Ireland's Own Library No. 3, Dublin, 1912), 29-30; *Grave and Gay Song Book* (Dublin, n.d.); James N. Healy, *The Mercier Book of Old Irish Street Ballads*, I (Cork, 1867), 243-5; *Ireland's Own*, 14 Nov. 1953, p. 11; P. J. McCall Broadside Collection National Library; 2 broadsides, National Library; Royal Irish Academy, 66.H.17; Trinity College, Dublin, Gall.R.15.35.

[22]IFC: 1592, pp. 127-31 (Cork, 1960).

[23]The materials I am gathering concerning this complex of legend and song are too vast to cite. I hope to publish a study of the complex.

[24]Georges-Denis Zimmermann, *Songs of Irish Rebellion* (Hatboro, Pa., 1967), 88-91.

[25]IFC: 633, pp 156-7 (Galway, 1939); Richard Sheil, *Sheil's Shamrock*, II (Dublin, 1840), 54-64; *Old "Come-all-Ye's,"* 2d ed. *(The Derry Journal,* Derry), 12; Trinity College, Dublin, Gall.R.15.34; 22.0.11; Pearse St. Library, Dublin, Irish Ballads No. 94; *Songs of Irish Civil Rights*, 12" LP, Outlet BOL 40008 (Belfast, ?1972).

[26]IFC 193, pp. 732-3 (Mayo, 1936); 329, pp. 155-8 (Mayo, 1936); 779, pp. 273-6 (Cork, 1940); 1064, pp. 581-2 (Kerry, 1943); S88 pp. 133-4 (Mayo, 1934); S461, pp. 539-42 (Kerry, ca. 1938); S576, pp. 202-5 (Tipperary, ca. 1938); S578, pp. 127-30 (Tipperary, Ca. 1938); S635, pp. 58-9 (Waterford ca. 1938); UCLA T5-69-46 (Cork via Clare, 1969); Zimmermann, 257-9; James N. Healy, *The Mercier Book of Old Irish Street Ballads*, III, 78-80; broadside, National Library.

[27]BBC 20216 (Cork, 1954). (Copies in IFC: disc 2266; UCLA T7-69-52). *Cf.* IFC: MacDonagh; Irish Ballad Book No. 1 (Copies in IFC and UCLA); *Ireland's Own*, 27 Sept. 1947, p. 12.

[28]See n. 19.

[29]IFC: 692, pp. 368-73 (Kerry, 1940); 789, pp. 58-60 (Cork, 1941); S288, pp. 192-4 (Cork, ca. 1938); S531, p. 162 (Tipperary, ca. 1938); P. J. McCall Broadside Collection 1, p. 121; broadside, National Library, Trinity College, Dublin, 21.bb.51, p. 143; cc.m.77; *Ireland's Own*, 31 May 1911, p. 5.

[30]IFC: MacDonagh and 17 other texts in the *Mss.*; Sam Henry Collection No. 164; P. J. McCall Broadside Collection, II, 119-21; broadside, National

Library; Royal Irish Academy, 66.H.17; *Ireland's Own,* 23 May 1917, p.
342; 16 Mar. 1929, p. 251; 30 Mar. 1935, p. 421.

[31]IFC: S209, pp. 55-60 (Leitrim); 921, pp. 475-8 (Cavan, 1943); 1441, pp.
401-04 (Kildare, 1956); *Home Rule Song Book* (n.p., n.d.); Healy, *Mercier
Book of Old Irish Street Ballads,* 1, 197-9; McCall Collection of Broadsides, 1, 144-45; 3 broadsides, National Library.

[32]IFC: 437, pp. 327-30 (Cork, 1937); 744, pp. 183-85 (Kerry, 1941); S679,
pp. 148-52 (Louth, ca. 1938); Tape 56D (Mayo, 1958); copy in UCLA
T7-69-54; Healy, *Old Irish Street Ballads,* 1, 194-7.

[33]IFC: MacDonagh; 1222, pp. 16-17 (Cavan, 1951); 1507, pp. 472-74
(Roscommon, 1958); S300, pp. 14-19 (Cork, ca. 1938); S1118, pp. 395-96
(Donegal, 1938); Healy, *Old Irish Street Ballads,* 1, 192-94; 2 broadsides,
National Library; Royal Irish Academy, 66.H.17.

[34]IFC: S48, pp. 205-07 (Galway, 1930); UCLA T7-69-43 (Donegal, 1969);
2 broadsides, National Library.

[35]IFC: S139, pp. 275-6 (Mayo, ca. 1938); S713, pp. 344-6 (Meath, 1938);
Colm O Lochlainn, *More Irish Street Ballads* (Dublin, 1965), pp. 166-7, 169
(from Sparling's *Irish Minstrelsy*); *Walton's Treasury of Irish Songs and
Ballads* (Dublin, n.d.), 113-14; *Walton's New Treasury of Irish Songs and
Ballads* (Dublin, c. 1968), 44-45; *In Dublin's Fair City* (Walton Songs,
Book 1; Dublin, n.d.), 44-5; *Sing an Irish Song,* Book 10 (Dublin, n.d.), 5-6.

[36]"Ballinagh Fire," IFC: S990, pp. 260-1, 293-94 (Cavan, 1938).

[37]I: IFC: MacDonagh; S239, pp. 161-02 (Roscommon, 1938). II: IFC:
S357, p. 317 (Cork, 1938). III: IFC: S357, pp. 207-08 (Cork, 1938); 347 pp.
5-7 (Kerry, 1938). IV: IFC: S448, pp. 187-8 (Kerry, ca. 1937).

[38]BBC LP24838 (Down, 1955).

[39]IFC: MacDonagh; 1757 (Sligo, 1969); S200, pp. 120-22 (Leitrim, 1938).

[40]IFC: 339, pp. 357-59 (Sligo, 1937); S182, pp. 663-67 (Sligo, ca. 1939);
S234, pp. 83-4 (Roscommon, 1938); S235, pp. 29a-31a, 43a-45a (Roscommon, 1938); S235, pp. 115-17 (Roscommon, 1938).

[41]IFC: 1190, pp. 427-30 (Mayo, 1950).

[42]Sam Henry, No. 585; BBC LP24837 (Down, 1955).

[43]IFC 521, pp. 75-88 (Galway, 1938); S253, pp. 405-21 (Roscommon, ca.
1938); S258, pp. 138-47 (Roscommon, 1937).

[44]Irish I: IFC: MacDonagh; UCLA T7-69-34 (Leitrim, 1969); Ranson,
128. Irish II: IFC: 736, pp. 493-535 (Cork, 1940). Irish III: IFC: Mac-
Donagh. Irish IV: IFC: S228, pp. 230-36 (Leitrim, 1938). Irish V: IFC 632,
pp. 603-06 (Kerry, 1939). Irish VI: *Ireland's Own,* 14 Aug. 1918, p. 101. Irish
VII: Broadside, National Library.

[45]Credited to Thomas Mozeen. See Croker (1839), 214-26, (1889),
204-15; Sheilds, "'*Some Songs and Ballads...,*'" 20; IFC: S912, pp. 38-43
(Wicklow, ca. 1938). (There are a number of broadside texts.)

[46]There was a local tradition that fairies used to play football in
Galroostown, Termonfeckin, Drogheda, County Louth, and used to take
a man named Dennis MacKeown to play with them. IFC: S674, pp. 140-42
(Louth, ca. 1936).

MAURICE HARMON

# Cobwebs before the Wind: Aspects of the Peasantry in Irish Literature from 1800 to 1916

EVEN THOUGH Ireland has been until quite recently predominantly an agricultural country, very few of her important writers have come from the peasant background or have made peasant life their major concern. Nevertheless, the sense of the rural background is particularly strong in modern Irish writing and in twentieth-century thinking about the development of modern Ireland.

The awareness of the peasant world emerges in James Joyce's *Portrait of the Artist* as a deprivation. As a product of the urban and east-coast culture of Dublin, Joyce was particularly conscious of the chasms of experience, culture, and language that separated him from the rural background. To Stephen Dedalus the peasants are attractive, holy, and mysterious. He listens with particular facination to Davin's story of that strange encounter with the peasant woman in the Ballyhoura Hills, in a section of the novel in which Joyce takes special care to emphasize Stephen's cultural and linguistic isolation:

The last words of Davin's story sang in his memory and

---

Maurice Harmon, Editor of the *Irish University Review: A Journal of Irish Studies,* teaches at University College, Dublin. He has been a visiting professor at American universities and has lectured widely in Europe. His best known works are *Sean O'Faolain; Modern Irish Literature: 1800-1967; J. M. Synge Centenary Papers* (ed.); and *With Darkness for a Nest: The Poetry of Thomes Kinsella, 1952-1973.*

the figure of the woman in the story stood forth, reflected in other figures of the peasant women whom he
had seen standing in the doorways at Clane as the
college cars drove by, as a type of her race and his own,
a batlike soul waking to the consciousness of itself in
darkness and secrecy and loneliness and through the
eyes and voice and gesture of a woman without guile,
calling the stranger to her bed.[1]

It may also be taken as a curious fact of Irish literary history
that the other founder of the modern prose tradition, George
Moore, should have entitled his book of stories about late
nineteenth-century rural Ireland *The Untilled Field* (1903),
as though nothing of value had been written and even
though Yeats had drawn attention to the importance of
William Carleton in 1889 in his introduction to his selection
of Carleton's stories. Granting that the Literary Revival was
generally weak in dealing with rural Ireland, tending to
transform peasants into angels in red petticoats, it is significant that for Moore, a sophisticated and experienced man of
letters, the task of depicting the peasantry still needed to be
done, and that Joyce found nothing that was useable in rural
Ireland, not even its literary expression. Joyce in fact ignores
the work of George Moore, which he knew, and the realistic
movement that had developed in the Abbey Theatre
through the plays of T. C. Murray, Padraic Colum, and J. M.
Synge. Together with William Carleton these writers
provide the main material for and consideration of the
realistic literary treatment of the Irish peasant in the period
from 1800-1916.

On the one side in nineteenth-century Ireland were
those Ascendancy writers, from Maria Edgeworth to Somer-
ville and Ross, whose approach to the peasants was circum-
scribed by cultural, racial, and religious barriers. On the
other were those few writers of ability, from William Carle-

ton to T. C. Murray, who took it upon themselves to present
the peasant in realistic terms in accordance with their own
natural understanding of peasant culture. In this general
division, J. M. Synge stands apart, in that he broke through
the barriers of the Ascendancy world and penetrated deeply
into the native, Catholic, and rural world.

The whole matter of the complex of classes and creeds
that made up late eighteenth- and early nineteenth-century
Ireland has been carefully outlined in Thomas Flanagan's
*The Irish Novelists, 1800-1850*.[2] It is unnecessary in this study
to survey the nineteenth-century Irish novel again, even for
evidence of its realistic treatment of the Irish peasant. My
aim is to take the created reality of William Carleton's
treatment of the peasant and—for the purpose of mutual
clarification—to place it side by side with other realistic
accounts of the peasant in late nineteenth-and early twentieth-century Irish literature. For the history of Anglo-Irish
literature, which may be said to have begun with Maria
Edgeworth and William Carleton, to grow toward Yeats,
Joyce, and the flowering of the Revival, then to taper off
into the literature of the post-revolutionary period, does not
in fact show a progressive deepening in the portrayal of the
Irish peasant. William Carleton stands unrivalled at the
beginning of a line that fades with his death in 1869, revives
with George Moore's single collection of short stories, shines
strongly in J. M. Synge, and thereafter—in the period outside our focus—emerges strongly in the work of Liam
O'Flaherty and Patrick Kavanagh.

Carleton's own, much-repeated claim that he wrote
with knowledge about the peasants is validated through his
best work: *Traits and Stories of the Irish Peasantry* (1830-33);
two or three good novels, *Valentine M'Clutchy* (1845), *The
Black Prophet* (1847), and *Emigrants of Ahadarra* (1847);
and his *Autobiography* (1896). No other writer of the nineteenth century can be placed in the same class, not John

Banim, whose *Peep O'Day* and *Crohore of the Billhook* flash with intermittent realism; whose best work, *The Collegians* (1847), is not about peasant life, and whose best short story, "Suil Dhuv" (1827), is too fragmented and lurid in the tradition of Banim; and not the romantic Boucicault.

The first point to be established about Carleton is that by birth and experience he was firmly rooted in Irish peasant life. He was born on a small farm in County Tyrone; as a storyteller, his father belonged to the oral tradition and had a prodigious memory, so that behind Carleton we have the sense of the bottomless mind of the storyteller. Furthermore, his father moved easily from Irish to English, although his mother felt more at home in Irish, as do Carleton's characters at moments of particular emotional intensity. Carleton was also fortunate in that the Clogher Valley, where he grew up, was rich in native culture:

> My native place is a spot rife with old legends, tales, traditions, customs and superstitions. . . . It was at home, however, and from my father's lips in particular, that they were perpetually sounding in my ears. In fact, his memory was a perfect storehouse, and a rich one, of all that the social antiquary, the man of letters, the poet, or the musician, would consider valuable. As a teller of old tales, legends, and historical anecdotes he was unrivalled, and his stock of them was inexhaustible. He spoke the Irish and English languages with nearly equal fluency. With all kinds of charms, old ranns, or poems, old prophecies, religious superstitions, tales of pilgrims, miracles and pilgrimages, anecdotes of blessed priests and friars, revelations from ghosts and fairies, was he thoroughly acquainted.[3]

As well as being an assertion of pride in Carleton's knowledge of his people, this is a claim made in the context of the whole antiquarian activity of the mid-nineteenth century. Carleton makes explicit reference to the work of George Petrie, Samuel Ferguson, and John O'Donovan. In other words, he knew that he wrote of a disappearing entity; he was within a movement that leads directly to the activities of Douglas Hyde, Lady Gregory, and W. B. Yeats, who in turn would recognize the value of the peasant background and would seek to record some of its culture.

Frank O'Connor has pointed out that *The Untilled Field* established some of the recurrent themes of modern Irish literature—rural insufficiency, anti-clericalism, and emigration.[4] But these are also part of Carleton's response, whose treatment of peasant society, while lacking Moore's greater literary awareness and sense of form, was nevertheless more profound and intimate. To place the two achievements side by side is to realize with considerable force how much had been lost between 1830 and 1903. Moore's advantages stem from his contacts with European and English literature; Carleton's stem from his immersion in his own material. And it is a revealing comment on what happened in between that Moore could regard his subject as virgin country.

Carleton's claim for the authenticity of his work is more than a question of home and environment. He is not the only Irish writer to assert the truthfulness of his own work. But he is the only Irish writer of his century to present his material in the kind of confident and complete manner that indicates the literary imagination in a fully creative relationship with its material. Again the contrast with Moore is instructive. Moore's stories are filtered through a defining and controlling intellect so that a basic idea holds the material together. Carleton writes in several voices and, while not all of these are successful and while the rational control is often weak, the emotional range and imaginative force are considerably greater than in Moore. We readily praise Carleton for his verisimilitude, for his realistic portrayal of the lives of the people, for the insight which he gives to their secret and often chaotic lives, for his personal experience of the church, the hedge-school, and the life of the poor scholar, for his knowledge of the pilgrimages, the stations, the weddings, Ribbonism, rackrenting, eviction, and peasant violence; on these levels his work is a record of the actual and the concrete. But his greatest claim to fame from the literary point of view, as distinct from the interest his work has for the historian and the folklorist, lies in those stories and those places in his best novels where he speaks out in mature control of his material.

An example of this may be found in "Going to Maynooth," which is a portrait of the artist as a young pedant and, like Joyce's later semiautobiographical novel, is written with an ironic and amused detachment even as it deals compassionately with a subject that is personal and painful. The story of the fair-haired boy, Denis, who is set aside by his family for the priesthood is a familiar one in Irish-Catholic experience. By use of the mock-serious tone Carleton achieves a degree of distancing through which he can freely reveal his own family background and his experiences as a young clerical scholar. The control comes from the mocking tone that enables Carleton to commemorate and judge at the same time, and to use the philomath English of the hedgeschool for the same dual purpose. His confident handling of his material and his casual, debunking humor appear in his description of Denis's father, nicknamed the Walking Pigeonhouse:

> He was quite straight, carried both his arms hanging by his sides, motionless and at their full length, like the pendulums of a clock that has ceased going. In his head, neck, and chest there was no muscular action visible; he walked, in fact, as if a milk-pail were upon his crown, or

as if a single nod of his would put the planets out of
order. . . . (II, p. 977)

The style serves both to illustrate and to undermine the
pedantic manner.

Carleton lightly and skillfully explains the attitudes
towards the Church and towards education that determine
and explain Denis's situation. A boy set aside for the priesthood, he says, "is cherished, humoured in all his caprices,
indulged in his boyish predilections, and raised above the
heads of his brothers, independently of all personal or
relative merit in himself. The consequence is, that he gradually becomes self-willed, proud, and arrogant, often to an
offensive degree. . . . " (II, p. 977) The story proceeds to
illustrate these observations in a series of broadly comic
scenes: the "pranks of pedantry," the verbal duels with his
father, the displays of learning for the neighbors, the
dalliance with the girls, the vanity of dress and deportment.
But Carleton's comic imagination also encompasses the
individual tragedy: Denis's progress, in part determined by
social pressures and conventions, in part by his own character, is not always consciously directed, so that the actual
consequences of his choice strike him only as he is about to
leave for Maynooth, when the decision made for him by
others and indulged in by himself, suddenly becomes a
reality. The conflict is made painfully apparent in those
tender scenes with Susan Connor, whom he had intended to
marry. Despite his capacity for warm human feelings, Denis
accepts the role to which he had become attached and
abandons the girl.

There is more to Denis than the flighty pedantry, as
Father Finnerty discovers when Denis tells him that he will
give him the colt in return for getting him into Maynooth but
makes it quite clear that the priest may have the colt on loan
until then. "He looked at me sharply," Denis proudly tells his

stunned and admiring family, "not expecting to find such
deep logic in one he conjectured to be but a tyro." (III, p.
992) No wonder the priest admits that Denis will be a useful
man in the church. It is in these extensions to the story that
Carleton brings social perspective to this comic portrait: in
the give and take between Denis and Father Finnerty, in the
family's generous celebration when he is pledged a place in
Maynooth, and in the subtle bargaining with the Bishop, in
whose palace he sees further evidence of material wealth. A
whole social canvas is built subtly and humorously around
the central figure.

"The Battle of the Factions" is a story in a different vein.
Here the mockery of "Going to Maynooth" is replaced by
another persona and a different tone. By presenting this
material through the authoritative and exuberant figure of
the teacher, Pat Frayne, Carleton achieves distance and
subtly allows the confident and sympathetic relationship of
narrator and story to be undermined by the actuality of his
narrative. At the same time, he uses Pat Frayne to provide a
delightfully casual and appreciative portrait of local girls
gossipping, a genial explanation of the differences between
a faction fight and a party fight, and a frame story of heroic
and romantic love. John O'Callaghan and Rose O'Hallaghan,
Carleton's Romeo and Juliet, fail to prevent the traditional                    ·
feud between their families and both die in a final tragic
tableau of the dead that concludes and diminishes Pat's
enthusiastic commemoration of the glory of the faction
fight. The result of this rich freight of incident, detail,
narrative, and tone is a powerful story of love and death,
custom adhered to with stupid principle, and family and
social life disrupted. All come naturally within the memory
of Pat Frayne, who, like the old soldier with no more wars to
fight, still hears the sounds of combat above the cries of loss
that also escape from his story. At the same time his tale,
being appropriate to the teller, reveals his own richly hu-
morous, extravert, and passionate nature.

Pat Frayne's impulse is to make a myth out of the faction fight. First of all, in a piece of superb description, he draws a clear distinction between the sectarian party fight, fought between Orangemen and Catholics, and the faction fight, fought between rival families. "In a party fight," he says,

a prophetic sense of danger hangs, as it were, over the crowd—the very air is loaded with apprehension; and the vengeance burst is preceded by a close, thick darkness, almost sulphury, that is more terrific than the conflict itself, though clearly less dangerous and fatal. The scowl of the opposing parties, the blanched cheeks, the knit brows, and the grinding teeth, not pretermitting the deadly gleams that shoot from their kindled eyes, are ornaments which a plain battle between factions cannot boast, . . . (II, p. 734)

A faction fight, he maintains, has none of this tragic and somber element. The atmosphere is light and comic:

Paddy's at home here, all song, dance, good-humor and affection . . . he tosses his hat in the air, in the height of mirth . . . He is, in fact, while under the influence of this heavily *afflatus*, in love with every one, man, woman, and child. If he meets his sweetheart, he will give her a kiss and a hug, and that with double kindness, because he is on his way to thrash her father or brother. . . . To be sure, skulls and bones are broken, and lives lost; but they are lost in pleasant fighting—they are the consequences of the sport, the beauty of which consists in breaking as many heads as you can. (II, p. 734)

This conversion of hate into love and violence into an acceptable mode of self-expression is appropriate to

Frayne's ritualizing imagination. The meeting of members
of opposing factions begins in a ritual of insult and challenge, an exchange of compliments prior to the exchange of
blows in what might well appear to be a lesser form of
duelling, more friendly, more informal, but just as deadly.
Frayne's exuberant dramatization of the actual fight begins
in a Dionysian delight: "The general harmony of this fine
row might be set to music," he observes and proceeds to
intermingle the sounds of language and cudgelling in a
merry crescendo. (II, p. 735) If the men are gleefully harmo-
nizing voice and cudgel, the women, he declares approv-
ingly, are "like heroines . . . fighting with amazing prowess
against their friends and relations." (II, p. 737) Their spe-
cialty is the "four pounder," a rock nestled in an apron or the
foot of a stocking and wielded effectively against the men.

Frayne happily commemorates scenes and deeds of
appalling violence with good-humored and appreciative
equanimity, but events overtake him and the tragic center of
the narrative becomes increasingly evident. Thus, when the
O'Hallaghans, driven weaponless into the cemetery, arm
themselves with the bones of the dead and re-emerge to
harrass their rivals, Frayne's enthusiasm falters. "God help
poor Ireland!" he exclaims, "when its inhabitants are so
pugnacious, that even the grave is no security against getting
their crowns cracked, and their bones factured!" (II, p. 738)
And in the final scene men crawl about, bloodied and
broken, women wail and curse, and even the triumphant
shouts of the victors are faint when compared to their initial
shouts. When, in the last stages of the battle, the young hero
is killed and Rose kills his murderer in a rage, then discover-
ing she has killed her own brother goes insane with this
double grief, the story's celebratory tone is finally defeated.
"It was truly dreadful," Frayne says somberly, describing
the death of John O'Callaghan,

even to the oldest fighter present, to see the strong rush of red blood that curvated about his neck, until it gurgled, gurgled, gurgled, and lappered, and bubbled out, ending in small red spouts, blackening and blackening, as they became fainter, and more faint. (II, p. 740)

The story, carried along by Frayne's rich nostalgia, has moved from the delightful social setting of the gossiping girls, to the church, to the rescue of Rose from the raging river by John, to the consequent reconciliation of the families, and to the inevitable and ultimately tragic breaking out of the quarrel once again. Like his grandfather, Frayne is opposed to the use of weapons in these fights. The sport requires that the deadlier instruments be avoided. If not, he concludes, with unconscious irony, faction fighting will degenerate to the level of party fighting.

The companion story, "The Party Fight and Funeral," although based on an actual fight that Carleton saw in Clogher at the age of twelve, lacks the power of Frayne's full-bodied and eloquent narrative, because Carlton speaks through the figure of a gentlemanly observer whose civilized opposition to what he describes turns the story into a moral document. Even the detailed description of the single-handed combat of Grimes and Kelly seems strained. In two places, however, the story breaks into life: once in the impassioned words of a fourteen-year-old boy over the body of his father, words repeated by all the relatives present, "by the God that's over me, if I live, night or day, I will not rest, till I have blood for blood, nor do I care who hears it, nor if I was hanged the next minute" (II, pp. 788-89); and once in the dramatic confrontation between the widow and the wife of his "murderer." The widow's curse, an authentic and powerful utterance made at the door of the "murderer," is more effective and alive than anything else in the story:

"Come out!" said the widow—"come out and look at
the sight that's here before you! Come and view *your
own* work! Lay but your hand upon the coffin, and the
blood of him you murdered will spout, before God and
these Christian people, in your guilty face! But, oh! may
the Almighty God bring *this home to you!*—May you
never leave this life, John Grimes, till worse nor has
overtaken me and mine fall upon you and yours! May
our curse light upon you this day!—the curse, I say, of
the widow and the orphans, that your bloody hand has
made us, may it blast you! May you, and all belonging
to you wither off of the 'airth! Night and day, sleeping
and waking, may you melt, until your name and your
place be disremembered, except to be cursed by them
that will hear of you and your hand of murdher! Amin,
we pray God this day!—and the widow and orphans'
prayer will not fall to the ground while your guilty head
is above it! Children, do you all say it?" (II, p. 791)

It is hard to believe that this terrible curse is made by a
woman who has opposed and cruelly suffered from the
sectarian bitterness of party fights. On an occasion like this
Carleton's mastery emerges and we sense his passionate
response to a system that turns men into savage beings and
destroys all finer feelings.

The whole question of violence in Carleton's work has
never been fully explored. Here the psychology of violence
forces a woman to perpetuate something she has consis-
tently opposed and to lay it as a sacred injunction on her
children, whom she has hitherto sought to protect from its
mindless control. Carleton's own detestation of violence is
based partly on his experience of the fight described in this
story, but more deeply still on his bitter and ineradicable
memory of the intrusion of Orangemen into his parents'
home in a spurious search for arms.

He has left one other study of sectarianism at work in the story "Wildgoose Lodge," which is an imaginative recreation of a reprisal execution that took place in County Louth. His account of the gathering of the Ribbonmen in a chapel and of the insane burning and killing of the whole family is a powerful indictment of violence. In one graphic incident a woman with flaming hair appears at a window of the burning house and shrieks for mercy. Carleton grimly notes that the only reply to this

> was the whoop from the Captain and his gang, of "No mercy—no mercy!" and that instant the former, and one of the latter, rushed to the spot, and ere the action could be perceived, the head was transfixed with a bayonet and a pike, both having entered it together. The word "mercy" was divided in her mouth; a short silence ensued, the head hung down on the window, but was instantly tossed back into the flames. (I. p. 942)

In Carleton's view the behavior of the Captain of the Ribbon Lodge is indicative of the demonic forces in human nature. The gathering in the chapel, the whiskey shared out like a communion, the sacrilegious oath-taking on the missal and on the altar, the utter bestiality of the killing of the Lynch family—an act of vengeance out of all proportion to the character of the man or what he had done—are all part of Carleton's vision of the satanic element in man.

This concept is endemic in Carleton, just as violence and anarchy seem to be endemic in all those nineteenth-century Irish novels that try to deal realistically with Irish peasant society. It might be conjectured that violence and anarchy are not so much realistic accounts of social reality as modes of moral judgment, metaphors of the moral imagination conceived in the face of a huge unmanageable evil. This literary recourse to the lurid may not be so much a result of the influence of the Gothic novel or the contemporary vogue of sensationalism, as a form of protest, produced in despair, against the massive, implacable, unchangeable system of landlordism, rackrenting, eviction, exploitation, injustice, famine, fever, death, and emigration. The real subject of these novels is not their visible world of savage murders and reprisals, nor the deceit, greed, and indifference to the landlords and their agents, but the predicament of a race so inhumanely denied a place in society or any glimmer of hope for the future.

Carleton's near obsession with the satanic individual, seen in "Wildgoose Lodge," "The Midnight Mass," and "The Lianhan Shee," becomes more pronounced in the novels. In *The Black Prophet*, O'Donnell the prophecy man is almost totally evil, a murderer pursued by nightmare, plotting evil, cruel, a man who has fallen from innocence. Solomon M'Slime and Valentine M'Clutchy in the novel *Valentine M'Clutchy* are Carleton's most obnoxious villains, utterly devoid of moral feeling, intent on their own greedy, cunning, and hypocritical exploitation of the people. Both of these powerful, if badly organized, novels are jagged acts of wrath against the system that denies and oppresses the people. Each is a succession of metaphors of action, characterization, and landscape for the amoral chaos to which Irish life had been reduced in the years leading to the Famine.

An apocalyptic sense of catastophe pervades *The Black Prophet*, which opens with a murderous quarrel between the prophet's daughter and her step-mother.

> The evening . . . had impressed on it a character of such dark and hopeless desolation as weighed down the heart with a feeling of cold and chilling gloom that was communicated by the dreary aspect of every thing around. . . . A brooding stillness, too, lay over all nature; cheerfulness had disappered, even the groves and

> hedges were silent, for the very birds had ceased to sing, and the earth seemed as if it mourned for the approaching calamity, as well as for that which had been already left. . . .
>
> . . . The sun, ere he sank among the dark western clouds, shot out over this dim and miserable prospect a light so angry, yet so ghastly, that gave to the whole earth a wild, alarming and spectral hue, like that seen in some feverish dream. In this appearance there was great terror and sublimity, for as it fell on the black shifting clouds the effect was made still more awful by the accidental resemblance which they bore to coffins, hearses, and funeral processions. . . . (I, p. 783)

The prophecy man himself is another image in this encompassing metaphor of doom; he is an embodiment of the evil which he forecasts.

But the extent and hopelessness of the calamity facing his people must have made the novelist's task virtually impossible. At his best in the short form, Carleton loses control frequently in the novels, where he works with a too-complicated plot, lurches into melodrama, and speaks directly to the landlord and the reader in lengthy asides that appeal for sanity, understanding, and justice. Flawed as works of art, the novels speak from the abyss to which his people have been driven and with a tone of utter hopelessness. Characters who make that symbolic pilgrimage from the rural desolation and the brink of death to the sumptuous world of Merrion Square on the assumption that, if they could only speak directly to the landlord in person, on the basis of their common humanity, their wrongs would be righted, are analogous to Carleton's own appeals within his novels for understanding. All are equally doomed. Owen M'Carthy staggers wearily home again only to find that the light of his life has died and his family has been evicted. Old

M'Mahon returns with an abject and doomed faith in the word of an Irish gentleman. There was no light and no redress, except in those unacceptable fictive solutions, those happy endings so dear to Carleton, at the end of *Valentine M'Clutchy*, at the end of "Tubber Derg," and at the end of *The Emigrants of Ahadarra*. In such fairytale endings wrongs are righted, the good are rewarded, and the kind landlord personally restores the land to the evicted. One wonders if Carleton knew how hollow the words sound at the end of *The Emigrants*:

> "M'Mahon," said Chevydale, "give me your hand. I am sorry that either you or your son have suffered anything on my account. I am come now to render you an act of justice—to compensate both you and him, as far as I can, for the anxiety you have endured. Consider yourselves both, therefore, as restored to your farms at the terms you proposed originally. I shall have leases prepared—give up the notion of emigration—the country cannot spare such men as you and your admirable son."
> (II, p. 639)

One ought to be able to read this as a savagely ironic comment, but Carleton lacks Swift's toughness of mind and temperament. Coming right after M'Mahon's sorrowful farewell to his buried wife, the landlord's words are stiff and lifeless. The true conclusion to these novels comes in the words of the prophet's daughter, a doomed protest made on an individual level but applicable to the whole people: "I tried to be good, but I'm only a cobweb before the wind—everything is against me, an' I think I'm like some one that never had a guardian angel to take care of them." (I, p. 893)

    Everything was against them and there were few angelic landlords. Ireland, Carleton truly said, "might be compared to one vast lazar-house filled with famine, disease and death."

> The very skies of Heaven were hung with the black drapery of the grave; for never since, nor within the memory of man before it, did the clouds present shapes of such gloomy and funeral import. Hearses, coffins, long funeral processions, and all the dark emblems of mortality were reflected, as it were, on the sky, from the terrible work of pestilence and famine, which was going forward on the earth beneath them. (I, p. 849)

His condemnation of the absentee landlord who abandoned his tenants to the rapacious agent erupts fiercely in his novels, but is given particular ironic edge in the letter of refusal sent by the agent Henry Hickman to the Right Honorable Lord Viscount Cumber in *Valentine M'Clutchy*. Hickman, a balanced and intelligent man, writes with scorn:

> "Should your tenantry ask me—'why are you this cruel and oppressive upon us?' what reply could I make but this—'I am cruel because his lordship is profligate. He wants more money to support his mistress, to feed her vanities and excesses, and you must endure distress and privation, that the insatiable rapacity of a courtezan may be gratified.'" (II, p. 159)

Hickman then advances a number of principles to the landlord, appealing in one that he remember that the peasants are human beings.

> " . . . they are susceptible of hunger, cold, grief, joy, sickness, and sorrow—that they love their children and domestic relatives, are attached to their religion, bound by strong and heartfelt ties to the soil they live on, and

are, in fact, moved by all those general laws and principles of life and nature, which go to make up social and
individual happiness. . . . " (II, p. 160)

The appeal is in vain. The novel itself is a bitter account of
rapacity and greed by the landlords and their agents, a
picture of almost total corruption, including the ruining of
women.

In *The Emigrants of Ahadarra,* Hycey has got two girls
into trouble and has designs on the servant, Nanny. In *The
Black Prophet,* Peggy Murtagh's parents refuse to forgive
her because she has had an illegitimate child, despite the
shame and guilt she feels. In that novel, too, the prophet
ascribes his own evil disposition to the effects on his character of his first wife's adultery. But it is in *Valentine
M'Clutchy* that the economic exploitation of the people is
specifically related to the sexual exploitation of girls. In this
novel the suspicion of sexual sin brings disgrace, parental
distress, and the loss of her fiance and friends to Mary
M'Laughlin. Sexual opportunism is presented as an aspect of
moral corruption: Solomon M'Slime tries to seduce Eliza the
barmaid; together with the libertine Phil M'Clutchy and
with the connivance of Valentine he responds lasciviously to
the young widow, Mrs. Tyrrell; and gains sexual success
with Susanna Wallace. And it is Poll Doolin's task to bring
illegitimate babies to the foundling hospital in Dublin.
Carleton's treatment of the theme of sexual exploitation and
the horror of sexual guilt among the people may be set
against his special feeling for innocent girls and in particular
for the bond between fathers and daughters, as in *The Black
Prophet* between O'Donnell and Sarah; in *The Emigrants of
Ahadarra* between old M'Mahon and Dora; in "Tubber
Derg" between Owen M'Carthy and his little girl; even Pat
Frayne's delighted portrait of the gossiping girls may be
regarded as suitably paternal.

In the face of the general oppression, so vividly presented in *Valentine M'Clutchy*, decent men are driven into
the Ribbon societies. At one meeting members bring forward their individual grievances to justify their actions.
"What have they left undone?" the leader asks, speaking of
the landlords, and proceeds to summarize what has been
said:

> "They have cheated you, robbed you, and oppressed
> you in every shape. They have scourged to death and
> transported your sons—and they have ruined your
> daughters, and brought them to sin and shame—sorrow
> and distraction. What have they left undone, I ax again?
> Haven't they treated yez like dirt under their feet?
> hunted yez like bloodhounds as they are—and as if ye
> were mad dogs? What is there they haven't made yez
> suffer?" (II p. 315)

There could hardly be any quick answer, unless we say
literally everything and look about for ten Carletons.

To move from William Carleton to George Moore is to
experience a strange sense of similarity, even as one begins
to realize that the differences are enormous. Although
Moore's themes are almost the same as Carleton's, the range
and intensity of his work are much reduced. Post-Famine
Ireland is a diminished reality, and the sense of vitality, of
masses of people lined up for a faction fight, crowding to
Midnight Mass, attending stations, going on pilgrimage,
getting married, abducting teachers, drinking, courting,
being evicted, emigrating, dying, is missing from Moore's
world, as it is from that of his contemporaries. I know of
nothing in Irish literature of the late nineteenth or early
twentieth century to match Carleton's sheer vitality and
sense of the density of human life.

Moore's restricted vision focuses generally on one of
two characters and his central theme is symbolically projected through a recurrent female figure—Lucy, Margaret
Dirken, or Julia Cahill. Opposed to them are not Carleton's
avaricious priests but a puritanical clergy who denounce
dancing, courting, and all natural expression—and encourage the made marriage. In "Home Sickness" Bryden returns
from New York to find health and peace in his own country.
By their dancing he and Margaret Dirken transform the
loneliness of the parish, but the oppressive quality of Irish
life impinges on his happiness: The people complain of the
bad times, the priest condemns the dancing, and Bryden
notices how obedient the people have become. Unable to
endure this new Ireland, he returns to America. In "Julia
Cahill's Curse," Father Madden, an authoritarian cleric,
represses the people. Opposed to him is the beautiful and
spirited Julia Cahill, who will not tolerate his interference,
whose beauty draws all men, but who is therefore denounced from the altar by the priest and forced to emigrate.
The legend of her curse lives on in the parish, a reason for its
fatal decline, and years later men set off for America to find
her and what she has come to represent.

But it is in his understated story, "The Exile," that
Moore portrays this devitalized Ireland most effectively. In
this sad story he deals with several interrelated themes at
once: the loneliness of Irish life, the insufficiency of rural
Ireland, and the necessity for emigration. The plot is simple.
Two brothers, Peter and James, live on a small farm with
their father. Peter is a gentle, uncertain man, not really suited
to farm work, who tries for the priesthood, then the police
force, then the priesthood again, and finally returns home to
the farm. James is a good farmer, loves Catherine and wants
her to marry him. Catherine, however, loves Peter and when
he enters the priesthood she joins a convent. When Peter
comes home, James emigrates and Catherine leaves the

convent to marry Peter. But the plot barely indicates what
the story is really saying. Exile is a general state, a condition
of existence, an absence. All the figures are in isolation from
each other; the impulses to do good add up to very little;
there is no sense of community, of a village, or of a parish, or
even of a person to whom one can reliably go for advice.
Ireland itself is in decay, as the descriptions of the landscape
also show, and human purpose has been so eroded that men
have no sense of direction and seem incapable of self-reliant
or creative action. Peter follows a number of callings; even
marriage holds little interest for him. James cannot get the
girl, so goes into exile in a final scene in which the implications of the story expand to include all the other figures at the
railway station waving sad farewells to their emigrants. It is
not a story that brings insight to the characters themselves,
but it tells us a great deal about their wasted, humorless, and
dispirited lives, about the loss of purpose, about the inade-
quacies of the background. Even the low-keyed style suits
the faint pulse of life in the story.

   It is no wonder that short-story writers in the post-
revolutionary period of disillusion and letdown should look
back to Moore, not just because he gave shape and design to
dominant and recurrent themes, but because he worked
with what they also had to work with—the diminished
reality of Irish life. Every man, a character in one of Sean
O'Faolain's stories, cries out in anguished loneliness, every
man lives out his own imagination of himself and every
imagination needs its background. The task that begins with
Moore is just that: to create an imaginative background and
to find a satisfying vision of life in an Ireland that the Famine
and the social and cultural changes that it brought about had
changed forever.

   In a memorable scene in Carleton's story "The Poor
Scholar," Dominick M'Evoy and his son James stand on a
bleak wintry hillside looking at the good land that had once

been theirs and so fierce is the son's sense of injustice that he
flings his spade aside and sets out to right the wrongs that
have been done to them:

> "To the divil I pitch slavery! An' now, father, wid the
> help o' God, this is the last day's work I'll ever put my
> hand to. There's no way of larnin' Latin here; but off to
> Munster I'll start, an' my face you'll never see in this
> parish, till, I come home either a priest an' a gintlemen.
> But that's not all, father dear, I'll rise you out of your
> distress, nor die in the struggle. I can't bear to see your
> gray hairs in sorrow and poverty."(II, p. 1076)

In the happy and unbearably moving ending to this story
Jimmy comes home a priest and has his father restored to a
comfortable living.

In reality, the process by which the people finally
gained possession of the land was long and bitter. By the end
of the nineteenth century, as a result of various land acts
ending in the Wyndham Act of 1903, the great change had
been effected. The soil of Ireland, as Padraic Colum phrased
it, passed from an alien landlordism into the hands of the
farmers themselves. The event is so momentous that it
comes out strongly in the literature: a matter of pride, as
Murtagh Cosgar says in Colum's *The Land*, thinking of what
had been gained and the legacy that would now pass to the
sons—"their manhood spared the shame that our manhood
knew. Standing in the rain with our hats off to let the
landlord—ay, or a landlord's dog boy—pass the way";[5] or,
as the old man in Daniel Corkery's *A Munster Twilight*
(1916) reminds his son, "You won't have to face what I had to
face, the struggling with landlords, and the law—the law,
that would leave a rich man poor and a poor man broken."[6]

The land, that had been won through a century of

struggle, becomes a dominant force in the realistic literature of the late nineteenth and early twentieth centuries, a cruel mistress to which men give their lives and their strength so that they can barely imagine the idea of a son who will not give himself to the same kind of existence. In T. C. Murray's play, *Birthright* (1910), Bat Morrisey would deny his eldest son's right to the farm and would send him into exile rather than see the land pass into the hands of a man not made in his own image and likeness: "The sweat o' my body an' my life is in every inch o' the land, and 'tis little he cares, with his hurling an' fiddling an' his versifying an' his confounded nonsense."[7] In Colum's *The Fiddler's House* (1903) the musician rejects the narrow life of the small farm for the freer life of the roads. And in his unpublished play, *The Kingdom of the Young*, the girl rebels against her father in favor of that joy in life that he and his generation had missed.

The choice facing the children of such harsh, authoritarian fathers, short of killing them with the blow of a loy, is to knuckle down to the brutalizing servitude of the small farm or to leave home. The basic irony of Colum's play *The Land* (1905), in which the action takes place on that great day in 1903 when the land is finally reclaimed and when men can walk upright at last, is that the victory turns to ashes in the mouth, that the conflict is now between slavery to the land and freedom for the self. The test of love and manhood is made in that context. Murtagh Cosgar is a hard man whose ten children have all emigrated, rejecting the farm in favor of opportunity elsewhere, just as Christy's brothers and sisters in *The Playboy of the Western World* have run from Old Mahon. His remaining son, Matt, declaring his love for Ellen, and finding that marriage to a girl who has neither land nor fortune is opposed by his father, first of all decides to seek freedom of action in America, but on reflection feels the pull of the land into which he has put so much of his strength. As a result he loses Ellen, who goes off to the new world with the other boys and girls, to "Streets and streets of houses and every house as crowded as the road outside the chapel when the people do be coming from Mass." (p. 128) Their images of America define what is missing from their lives in rural Ireland: fine clothes, crowded streets, great houses, money, marriage, opportunity, theaters, fine things, and above all—personal freedom!—not "houses in bogs and fields." (p.128)

The dominant issues in late nineteenth-and early twentieth-century Irish writing about the peasants are land hunger, loneliness, repression, individual freedom of action, family and personal pride. Carleton had written of a huge and impersonal tragedy and of events sometimes so anarchical as to be almost melodramatic. The later writers focus on issues of individual choice and the pressures of a tight society.

Possession of the land brought economic and social stresses which in turn affected personal decision. Denis O'Shaughnessy could go off to Maynooth on a genial wave of vanity and family pride; he could even return to marry Susan Connor without experiencing either personal guilt or family opposition. Indeed, since most spoiled priests seem to have become hedge-school teachers, a position inferior only to the priest, the idea of returning from Maynooth seems to have been quite acceptable. But in late nineteenth-century Ireland the way back was much harder.

Maurice Harte, in T. C. Murray's play of the same title, in what is the typical modern instance, found the whole experience traumatic. His honest realization that he has no vocation is disastrous for himself, for his brother, who has made a good match and whose wedding ceremony is to be performed by Maurice, and for his family, who have gone deeply in debt to pay for his education on the strength of one day having a priest in the family. Act One ends with their determined effort to dissuade him from his decision to leave Maynooth:

| | |
|---|---|
| Mrs. Harte. | Will you be talking wild, frightening, foolish talk about your conscience, and not think at all of them, nor of us, and all we done for you? |
| Maurice. | *(distressfully)*. Mother! Mother! |
| Mrs. Harte. | You'll go back? 'Tis only a mistake? |
| Maurice. | Great God of Heaven! . . . you'll kill me. |
| Michael. | You'll go back, Maurice? The vocation will come to you in time with the help o' God. It will, surely. |
| Maurice. | Don't ask me! Don't ask me! |
| Owen. | 'Twould be better for you, Maurice. 'Twould surely. |
| Mrs. Harte. | *(passionately)*. If you don't how can I ever face outside this door or lift up my head again? |
| Maurice. | *(piteously)*. Mother! |
| Mrs. Harte. | How could I listen to the neighbours making pity for me, and many o' them only glad in their hearts? How could I ever face again into the town o' Macroom? |
| Maurice. | Oh, don't. |
| Mrs. Harte. | I tell you, Maurice, I'd rather be lying dead a thousand times in the graveyeard over at Killnamartyra— |
| Maurice. | (with a sudden cry). Stop, mother, stop! (There is a tense pause.) I'll . . . I'll go back—as—as you all wish it. |

*He sinks into a seat with an air of hopeless dejection.*
> Mrs. Harte.   *(drawing a long deep breath).*
>               God bless you, boy, for that! I
>               knew you would.
> Owen.         'Tis the best thing, surely.
> Mrs. Harte.   *(kneeling).* Oh, thanks be to the
>               Almighty God and His Blessed
>               Mother this day![8]

Not unexpectedly, Act Two ends with the final return
of Maurice from Maynooth, broken by this terrible conflict.
Murray's dramatization of the conflict is superbly accurate
in its insight into the mixture of ignorance, pride, love, and
determination in the family that compels the sensitive young
cleric to go against his own conscience. Significantly, his role
in this scene is reduced to anguished cries, since there is no
way that he can hope to explain his inner torment to his
peasant family and since he himself knows only too well the
force of respectability that drives them to oppose him.
Ironically, his parents offer prayers of praise and thanksgiv-
ing to a God whom they see on the side of the small farmer.

The issues of respectability and social status have become central: in T. C. Murray, in Lennox Robinson's *The
Clancy Name*, in which another dominating parent fights to
hold both land and honor for her son, in Padriac Colum's
fiercely proud possessors of land. Once sounded, the theme
echoes forward to O'Connor and O'Faolain and into all
those novels, stories, and plays in post-revolutionary Ireland
that deal with the middle class. Not that it has been entirely
absent from Carleton, as, for example, in that harsh story of
greed and cunning that comes after his essay on "The
Geography of an Irish Oath," but it is essentially a product of
that social revolution by which men, finding secure possession of the land, turn to other goals for themselves and their
children—respectability,   position,   wealth,   the   good

match, the secure profession, and the drying of the marrow from the bone.

To move through the work of George Moore, Padraic Colum, and T. C. Murray toward J. M. Synge is to see how central Synge was to the prevailing mood. His work is not so much the rushing up of the buried fire, as Yeats had declared, nor even that he was in advance of his time, as Yeats also said—seeing him mainly within the context of nationalistic conflict and narrow-minded opposition—but that he had the capacity to portray more deeply and with greater clarity the essential psychological and social problems of the time. To place his work beside any of these contemporaries is to see its greater vitality and imaginative force. His first play, *In the Shadow of the Glen,* takes the familiar custom of the made marriage and shows the utter loneliness of the spirit to which it may lead. It is to be free of this kind of bargain that Colum's young people empty out of the countryside and it is in obedience to its harsh law that the less spirited couple, Sally and Cornelius, accept the marriage compact in return for the farm for themselves and their children. Cornelius's final words provide an ironic curtain: "Men of Ballykillduff . . . stay on the land, and you'll be saved in the man and in the nation. The nation, men of Ballykillduff, do you ever think of it at all? Do you ever think of the Irish nation that is waiting all this time to be born?"[9]

It is tempting to pursue an answer to this question as to the kind of nation born out of such peasant practicality and compromise, or from a society from which the best have fled. The consideration would lead us right into the gombeen paradise of post-revolutionary Ireland and through the realization that, although the Easter Rising of 1916 was led by poets and schoolteachers and that although romantic nationalism gained the day in the immediate aftermath, it was the peasants in the towns and cities who won the social revolution as they flooded into the jobs and took over.

Here, more immediately, we may note the judgement
of the final scene in *In the Shadow of the Glen*,[10] after Nora
Burke has chosen the freedom of the roads, in which her old
husband sits down with her spineless young man who had
hoped by his death and through marriage with Nora to get
the money and the land:

> Dan      *(throwing away his stick)*. I was
> thinking to strike you, Michael
> Dara, but you're a quiet man,
> God help you, and I don't mind
> you at all.

> *(He pours out two glasses of whisky, and gives one to
> Michael.)*

> Dan.      Your good health, Michael Dara.
> Michael.      God reward you, Daniel Burke,
> and may you have a long life,
> and a quiet life, and good health
> with it.

> *(They drink.)*

> Curtain.
> (p.118)

Of the two choices made, Nora's is the more attractive,
even though it perhaps leads to bad health and a short life.
Furthermore, it is in line with the choices made in *Birthright*,
in Moore's stories, in *The Fiddler's House*, and in *The
Kingdom of the Young*. What the restrictive life of the made
marriage and the small farm may involve is projected all
through *In the Shadow of the Glen* as social and sexual
deprivation and imaginative loss. It is this kind of existence
that the young people in Colum's *The Land* want to avoid.
Carleton saw the huge and general catastrophe of the

whole people. Synge, Colum, Moore, and Murray see the tragedy of the individual and the particular. "No man at all," Maurya concludes sadly and firmly in *Riders to the Sea*, "can be living forever and we must be satisfied." (p. 97) The application is universal but Synge has moved toward it through an austere and classical discipline so that the individual instance becomes representative of all. Perhaps the most fundamental aspect of Synge's best work is his ritualizing ability. In his hands the issues of the made marriage, the doomed existence, the rebellion against the old, and the familiar figures of the spineless young men, the spirited girls and the crusty old men, are transformed into a ritualizing and ritualized existence in which every gesture and every action become formalized and are made part of a myth.

The triumph of Synge's art and its illusion of absolute realism and fidelity to peasant life is that it translates reality into the mythical. Pegeen Mike and her transforming Christy Mahon speak of love's experience with pristine wonder and delight. In the glorification of the potential hero, resurrection is a poetic fact, a comic correlative for a life-giving spirit by which the play itself, its language, its action, and its central figures transcend themselves and are lifted out of the here and the now. The social reality remains the impoverishment of the Congested Districts, a world of emigration and purposelessness, of spineless humanity, of the made marriage, of a desolation much grimmer than anything in Colum or Moore. That Christy may go romancing through a romping lifetime to the dawning of the Judgement Day only means that he exists in the myth created by the play. In that world, redeemed by the imagination, the killing of one's da is as acceptable and as real as Pat Frayne's enthusiastic celebration of murder by faction. Ultimately it may be said that what makes Carleton and Synge the great artists that they are is that in their best work imagination triumphs over reality and the inherent calamities of life are transcended.

Synge penetrated the peasant culture, but Carleton possessed it, and for both the individuality of Irish life was diminishing. Carleton's consciousness of this decline stimulated him to be the memorialist of his people and in this he resembled his contemporary poets and antiquarians and anticipated the various movements of cultural and literary renewal of the Revival period. For whether we discuss Irish writing in terms of the east-west dichotomy or the present-past division, the central impulse in the majority of the writers is to create out of loss, in the face of the steady erosion of that network of values, responses and customs that make a distinctive culture. Because of this inherent anemia, Yeats felt his isolation within a tradition that was broken. From his romantic viewpoint rural Ireland was "a community bound together by imaginative possessions, by stories and poems which have grown out of its own life, and by a past of great passions which still waken the heart to imaginative action."[11] The words echo Carleton's evocation of life in the Clogher Valley at the end of the eighteenth century, although they conveniently ignore what had been lost in the meantime.

Even Joyce, repenting in Europe, could send Gabriel Conroy's thoughts drifting westward across the Shannon, to where Synge had found a "popular imagination" that was "fiery and magnificent, and tender"[12] and to where Douglas Hyde had found "one of the most valuable heritages of the Irish race—its Folk Songs" among "the Irish-speaking peasantry—a class which is disappearing with alarming rapidity."[13] Even for later realistic writers, peasant Ireland has been a region of the imagination and of the spirit through which they sought contact and tried to come to terms with remnants of the old Gaelic way of life and the lost childhood of the race. Affronted by the middle-class world of post-revolutionary Ireland and later still by the mid-Atlantic culture that further threatened and diminished the individuality of Irish life, they made imaginative pilgrimages on the long road to Ummera, to the silence of the valley in Gougane Barra, to Clonmacnoise crossed with light, to the chosen island of Granuaile, to the allegorical waters at Ballydavid Pier, to the shards of a lost culture in the rough field. Even George Moore's artists, although resentful of local irritations, knew that imaginative nourishment lay in what Paddy Durkin and Father Pat would say to them on the roadside. "One explores an inheritance to free oneself and others. . . . But one must start from home—so the poem begins where I began myself, with a Catholic family in the townland of Garvaghey, in the country of Tyrone, in the province of Ulster"[14]—which is where the story began with Carleton.

[1]James Joyce, *A Portrait of the Artist as a Young Man* (New York: Viking Press, 1964), p. 183.

[2]New York: Columbia University Press, 1959.

[3]*The Works of William Carleton* (New York: P. F. Collier, 1881), II, 645.

[4]*A Short History of Irish Literature* (New York: Capricorn Books, 1968), pp. 196-98.

[5]Padraic Colum, *Three Plays* (New York: Macmillan, 1925), p. 115.

[6]Daniel Corkery, *A Munster Twilight* (Dublin: Talbot, 1916), p. 85.

[7]T. C. Murray, *Birthright* (Dublin: Maunsell, 1911), p. 14. Page references provided in the essay where dates refer to first performances.

[8]T. C. Murray, *Maurice Harte* (Dublin: Maunsell, 1911), pp. 38-39.

[9]Padraic Colum, "The Land" in *Three Plays*, p. 47.

[10]*The Complete Works of John M. Synge* (New York: Random House, 1935). Page references provided in the essay.

[11]W. B. Yeats, "The Great Plains," *Ideas of Good and Evil* (Dublin: Maunsell, 1907), p. 337.

[12]J. M. Synge, *The Complete Plays*, "Preface," p. ix.

[13]Douglas Hyde, "Preface," *Love Songs of Connacht* (Dublin: Gill and Son, 1905), p. v.

[14]John Montague, "Note to *The Rough Field*," *The Rough Field* (Dublin: Dolmen, 1972).

# Peasants and Emigrants: Considerations of the Gaelic League as a Social Movement

ALTHOUGH A PEASANT is defined as "one who lives in the country and works on the land, either as a small farmer or as a laborer,"[1] the term connotes stasis and what David Riesman has called "tradition direction."[2] The tendency to romanticize the "spiritual qualities of the peasantry"[3] has asserted itself in both imaginative and social science literature, usually with the objective of counterposing the non-economically determined ethos of the peasant to the crassness of "economic Man." Yet when we turn our attention to so rural a society as nineteenth-century Ireland, we find that change and profit are fundamental to any satisfactory sketch that might be drawn. Just prior to the famine of the 1840s Ireland contained approximately 800,000 agricultural holdings, not counting over 135,000 holdings of less than one acre.[4] Over sixty percent of the holdings of one or more acres were not larger than fifteen acres; market-oriented agriculture was restricted by the limited use of cash and by poor transportation. By 1910 the number of holdings had declined by nearly 300,000 and those of from one to fifteen acres accounted for only forty-one percent of the smaller total. The number of farm laborers whose subsistence in the earlier period was often aided by tiny conacre plots had

Martin J. Waters (deceased) was Associate Professor of History at Cooper Union. His recent research on the rise of nationalism in Ireland has led to the formulation of the thesis that is explored in his essay.

dwindled from 1,326,000 to 277,000; the population of the country as a whole had declined by four millions.

In effect, the nineteenth century witnessed a massive social transformation characterized by larger holdings increasingly organized in response to market demands, the operation of which was facilitated by the growth of banking and the development of railroads. This change was reflected in emigration statistics and in the decline of tillage and the growth of pasturage, a prerequisite for an enormous increase in the exportation of cattle to Britain. Aside from linking the Irish economy more closely to Britain's, the net result "was to substitute a rural bourgeoisie for a rural proletariat,"[5] and few aspects of Irish life—whether religious, political, literary, or marital—were unaffected. The notion, then, of an "Irish peasantry" with a peculiar ethos somehow remaining outside the dynamics of Irish history, except in the sense of its vanishing through emigration or of its being fundamentally modified through the adoption of a market orientation, is untenable.

One aspect of the activities of those who emigrated will be considered below while, for those who remained, there is no doubt that the material conditions of life improved markedly. By the early twentieth century the Irish farmer was secure in his tenure, and endemic starvation was a thing of the past. The cost of this achievement was great, not only in terms of the political struggles, but in terms of social and personal discipline required to maintain a claim to the land in the face of great adversity. At the turn of the century a sense of devitalization pervaded the Irish countryside, for the imperatives of survival dovetailed well with late (and arranged) marriages, clerical puritanism, and continued emigration of the young and adventurous. Thus, acquisitiveness and repression, tenacity and dullness, relative prosperity and the loss of cultural identity were the mixed legacy of the post-Famine struggles.

The Gaelic League was but one of a number of responses to the state of affairs, but because of its widespread
social and intellectual impact, it was perhaps the most
important. As an historical phenomenon it is a somewhat
curious case since everyone pays obeisance to it while no
one studies it in depth. It is generally agreed that the League
had a powerful impact on Irish history, even if no systematic
attempt has been made to describe its progress as an organization or to discover what kinds of people were inclined to
play an active role in its affairs. Nor has there been much of
an attempt to relate the growth of the Gaelic League and,
more generally, the development of ideological nationalism
in Ireland to changes in the Irish social structure. What
follows is, then, an effort to outline the League's early
development, and to consider in terms of their social backgrounds, a part of the first and second echelon leadership of
the movement.

The evidence on the growth of the Gaelic League is
somewhat inconclusive. However, it provides a fairly sharp
outline which may temporarily diminish misgivings about
its lack of comprehensiveness. For instance, when we read
in the Executive Committee Minute Book for July 7, 1897,
that "the Secretary was authorized to buy a regular minute
book,"[6] we immediately recognize that four years after its
foundation, the League was still a small and informal body
of enthusiasts. The impression is confirmed by a claim that
the Gaelic League branch established in Farney in 1895 was
one of the first half dozen in Ireland.[7] Nor does the fact that
it was three years before a branch was established in London
contradict the impression.[8] It seems a safe assumption that
during its early years the Gaelic League did not spread like
wildfire.

The popular movement to the League appears to have
begun in 1899; at the end of that year it had 107 fully
affiliated branches. Most of the growth represented by this

figure seems to have occurred during 1899 when the League adopted a new constitution.[9] However, the 107 branches represented only the threshold of spectacular growth. By February of 1901 there were over two hundred branches, and there were nearly four hundred the year after that. The circulation of *An Claidheamh Soluis,* the weekly newspaper of the League, more than doubled, to 4,000 readers, in the eighteen months after July, 1900. In addition, the disbursement of revenues increased enormously over the same period. For the six months extending from June 8, 1899, to January 2, 1900, the League had receipts of £1109.19.11; whereas in January and February, 1902, receipts totalled £955.3.2. The growth indicator is even more impressive when it is noted that in the second half of 1899, £450 of the League's receipts were in the form of windfall gifts—from Patrick Ford of the New York *Irish World* and from the Buenos Aires Branch of the League. And expenditures for the second half of 1899 were £655.10.2, while for the first two months of 1902 they were £967.11.9. This growth forced the League to change its organizational pattern. While up to that time, it remained an essentially voluntaristic organization, it now required a full-time, salaried secretary as well as a salaried newspaper editor.[10]

Unfortunately, the evidence does not provide any long-sought solutions to troublesome questions regarding Irish history and culture. Indeed, it is disconcerting because it calls one traditional view into question, in that it suggests that the emergence of Irish cultural nationalism on a broad scale may have less to do with the deposition of Charles Stewart Parnell as leader of the Irish Party by a group of politicians sitting in a Westminster Committee Room than it had to do with what was happening in Ireland. Generally we are told that disillusionment over the fall of Parnell led Irishmen away from political and into literary and cultural concerns. P. S. O'Hegarty's view is typical, though perhaps more extravagantly expressed than most:

The spirit of Ireland, the spirit that maintained the
Underground Nation in its underground dungeon and
pushed it out, and maintained it outside, had given
Parnell's policy a trial.... And with the death of Parnell
it had gone to ground again, fashioning a new policy.[11]

It is true that Celticism became a popular literary mode in
the nineties, but this was hardly a movement with a broad
social or political base. The slow progress of the Gaelic
League in its early years suggests that its later growth had
little to do with the fall of Parnell. It seems more useful to
raise two other questions: Was anything happening at the
turn of the century that made the Gaelic League attractive to
large numbers of Irishmen? Was the growth of the League in
this period related to any long developing trends?

With regard to the first question I would suggest that
the Boer War provided a crucial catalyst to the development
of Irish cultural nationalism because it raised directly the
question of whether it was possible to be simultaneously an
Irish nationalist and a British imperialist. The goals of the
Home Rule Party were quite utilitarian at this time, and their
arguments were based on the premise that unless Ireland
received justice in the form of Home Rule, she would
inevitably be a sullen and badly governed country.[12] John
Redmond, in fact, was a not-very-secret admirer of Cecil
Rhodes,[13] and leading Irish M.P.s were embarrassed by
enthusiastic expressions of pro-Boer sentiment (i.e., cheer-
ing British defeats) by Parliamentary underlings.[14] The Parliamentarians, after all, had to persuade the dominant British
that Home Rule would be good for them as well as for the
Irish, and this necessarily involved deemphasizing differences between the two islands for the sake of showing that
the Irish were as "fit" for Home Rule as were the British.
Beyond that there was no particular reason to suppose that
Irishmen could not be loyal supporters of the British Em-

pire. This orientation, however sensible, could exact a high emotional price, at least for some. What did it mean to be Irish if Home Rule were to be achieved by demonstrating how like the British the Irish were? The Boer War did not create this tension, but it acted as the catalyst for many people. The cultural nationalism propounded some years earlier by Douglas Hyde in his address on "The Necessity for de-Anglicizing the Irish Nation"[15] suddenly became relevant to the needs of quite large numbers of Irishmen. In 1900 D. P. Moran established the Dublin *Leader,* which preached what he called "Irish-Irelandism" in a trenchant way, and its success was indicative of a new culturally militant mood among the Catholic middle classes.

Obviously, this affinity for cultural nationalism did not spring from nowhere. There were, of course, the literary traditions of relatively long and recent standing: the Gaelic, the Anglo-Irish, the Young Ireland, and the Celtic Revival. But acquaintance with these (or at least the last three) presupposed literacy in English, and the decline of the Irish illiteracy rate from fifty-three percent to sixteen percent between 1841 and 1901 was a crucial prerequisite for the development of any broad based movement of cultural nationalism.[16] Literacy increased the opportunities of large numbers of Irishmen to acquaint themselves with a national-ist version of the Irish past through propaganda and histor-ical romances in the popular press. Yeats speaks with some misgivings of young men in the 1890s, enthusiasts for Irish literature of a sort, who spent their spare time in the library reading back copies of the *Nation,*[17] and while these were few in number, variants of the *Nation* tradition of patriotic history and romance were carried forward by many news-papers and many magazines in the second half of the nineteenth century.[18] Ironically, then, though Gaelic Lea-guers later attacked the national schools for undermining the position of the Irish language, these same schools, by creating a peasantry literate in English, helped to forge a national consciousness that had not been so pervasive in the first half of the century.[19]

A second effect of increased literacy was greater opportunity for mobility, both social and geographical. The literate children of peasants could become teachers, civil servants, journalists, and priests. Or they could make use of their civilized graces[20] to seek their fortunes in London, New York, and elsewhere. For emigrants the experience of an alien environment often had the effect of heightening national consciousness. The sense of remoteness encouraged a tendency to think of Ireland in terms of its unity rather than its diversity; the nation rather than the parish became the emotional focal point. Moreover, the leaving of one's native place and perhaps one's original social class, when combined with the coldness and even hostility of the new environment contributed to the development of an emotional need to cluster with one's own kind and to rebind broken ties by consciously articulating a communal and national identity.[21] A London Gaelic Leaguer very aptly summed up the situation for himself and for many others like him when he remarked that the Gaelic League gave him an opportunity to

> Stand awhile amongst kindred spirits, who live for an Idea in a vast city whose current of life is foreign to them and you. . . . Every working Gaelic Leaguer in London must feel that his daily life is worsted; but there is a certain recovery of self, a certain intensity of feeling, a sudden harmonization of life at the great gatherings of the League. At last, so to say, you seem to live in tune with Nature.[22]

These considerations become significant when we recognize that returned emigrants played an important role in the development of the Gaelic League and, more generally, the Irish-Ireland movement. Indeed, the term "Irish-Ireland" was coined by D. P. Moran who had spent many years in England before returning to Ireland in 1900. As an Irishman in London he was appalled by the cultural pretensions of the British and their West Briton imitators. At the same time, as one who had developed the personal qualities requisite for success in a foreign place, he was disturbed by what he regarded as a lack of vitality, initiative, and backbone in his countrymen who had stayed at home. In his view, the Irish people were "secretly content to be a conquered race," and their enthusiasm at political meetings, far from being a sign of vitality, was in reality "a delirious burst of defiance on a background of sluggishness and despair."[23] The only remedy for this state of affairs was an increase of self-respect, and this could be achieved on personal and national levels only through cultural revival, with the native language serving as the core of a new national self-image, and through economic revival which would be achieved by the widespread practice of thrift, industry, and sobriety—the qualities which characterized successful Irishmen abroad. Moran was one of the more factious Irish-Irelanders, but his linking of cultural nationalism with a somewhat dated economic modernism was far from unique.

Moreover, though Moran was not, many of the immigrants who returned had been peasants before they left Ireland, though not necessarily impoverished ones. Hardly any attempt has been made to see the Gaelic League and the Irish-Ireland movement as a response to changing Irish social structure. F. S. L. Lyons in his recent history of *Ireland Since the Famine* has stressed the vast social changes of the nineteenth century, and he has devoted a whole chapter to the Irish-Ireland movement,[24] but he has not succeeded in integrating the two. The evidence presented here is suggestive rather than definitive, but hopefully it will at least provide a basis for further consideration of the question. The most important source for this attempt at integration is a series of biographical sketches which appeared in the *Irish Peasant* in 1906. The *Peasant*, as the paper was usually called, was published in Navan, and it was edited by W. P. Ryan, a Tipperary-born London journalist and an ardent Gaelic Leaguer, who had returned to Ireland at the end of 1905 to take up the editorship.[25] Ryan immediately recast the paper in an Irish-Ireland mold, and in one of the new features, called "Irish Pioneers," he highlighted the contributions of various people to the Gaelic Revival. Fifty-two sketches appeared before Michael Cardinal Logue's disapproval of the paper's views on educational and other questions forced it to cease publication in Navan.[26] Not all the "Pioneers" were Irish-Irelanders,[27] and although there are gaps in the file, it is still possible to identify thirty-one (counting Ryan himself) who were clearly committed to the Gaelic League or the Irish-Ireland movement or both.

The group included seven civil servants, four journalists, four gentlefolk writers, three businessmen, three Catholic priests, two teachers, and one each of the following: Protestant clergyman, lawyer, doctor, engineer, farmer, school monitor, shop assistant, and one whose occupation was unknown. Though it spans a wide spectrum, the group as a whole seems solidly Catholic and middle class. Perhaps three of the group were Protestant.[28] With respect to geographical mobility, at least seventeen can be classified as emigrants, and twelve of these became involved in the movement while out of Ireland. (An emigrant is here defined as one who earned his living outside of Ireland for a substantial period of time. People who had travelled in foreign parts, like Douglas Hyde or William Gibson, are not included in this category.) Of the fourteen who had not emigrated, all but three had either migrated within Ireland, travelled to foreign places, or both. Of the three who had not moved about very much, two were Catholic Parish Priests who had attended diocesan seminaries. Nineteen are explicitly identified as having been educated beyond the National School level, and five of these had attended a university. Two more probably went beyond the National School level. Of the other ten, four were civil servants, three were employed by the Gaelic League, one was a National School teacher, one was a journalist, and one a businessman. All but one of these ten had been an emigrant.

Though the most heavily represented occupations (civil servants—seven, priests—three, businessmen—three, journalists—four, teachers—two, make up nineteen of the thirty-one) were accessible to upwardly mobile peasants, it is possible only to make a guess about which members of the group had come from peasant stock—at least if we are to avoid the conclusion that everyone who was not a gentleman was a peasant. For the moment, I have assumed that anyone who went to a university was not a peasant. Positive clues were whether place names of points of origin were Irish, whether these points were identified in terms of the diocesan or parochial affiliation, and whether parents were Irish speakers. On this basis probably sixteen were peasants, probably thirteen were not, and two could not be classified.

Some examples may clarify the confusion: I have identified Sean O'Ceallaigh as a peasant even though his father was a quite prosperous farmer with over two hundred acres; on the other hand, he came from the island of Valentia, and he spoke Irish from youth. When Thomas Flannery was a small boy, his Irish-speaking parents migrated to Manchester after having been evicted from their holding; he grew up in a large city, but he was clearly of peasant background. W. P. Ryan, by contrast, is a simple case. His family was twice evicted from holdings, he grew up near Templemore, Tipperary, and he did not go to England until he was nineteen. R. O'Neill Russell's background was rural, but his family are identified as being graziers, so he does not qualify. Obviously, there were many gradations, cultural, social, and economic in the Irish countryside, and although the evidence as well as the very concept of peasant is problematical, it seems fair to conclude that most members of the group were not far removed from the peasantry in terms of their social origins. Of the sixteen identified as being of peasant origin, five were civil servants, two were journalists, two were teachers, two were priests, and five were employed by the Gaelic League (the previous occupations of the Gaelic League employees had been school monitor, shop assistant, businessman, farmer, and unknown).

The crucial point is that none was a peasant any longer. The whole group was highly mobile in geographical and social terms; they had broken bonds of place and class; they were also frustrated by their new circumstances. This was certainly true of Ryan and Moran, who could never fully acclimate themselves to being journalists in the heart of the British Empire—or to the Anglo-Irish hegemony over cultural matters; eventually they both returned to Ireland to preach the Irish-Ireland gospel.[29] There are scattered references in Ryan's sketches to the frustrations of civil servants who had "dropped into" their careers,[30] and of one Ryan commented that "had there been no language movement he would never have found the fit sphere for his qualities and powers."[31] In general the sketches convey an image of energetic and moderately successful men whose careers provided inadequate scope for their talents and ambitions. The Irish-Ireland movement offered them the hope of participating in something new and grand, something that provided a sense of high purpose as well as the hope that their true merits and sacrifices would be recognized and appreciated. Such men were crucial to the making of modern Ireland—a development that some have traced to the still relatively uncharted valley that lies between the twin peaks of Parnell's fall and the Easter Rising.[32]

The people in this group were not especially typical of the population of Ireland, nor even of the whole Gaelic League membership. Rather, they represented a significant leadership element within the Irish-Ireland movement. Their motives for becoming active in the movement were highly tinged with a desire for self-respect, but there were other reasons for joining the League; not the least of these was the opportunity it offered for social contact between the sexes. The correspondent for the *Peasant* put the matter directly when he welcomed the reopening of Irish classes in the fall of 1905:

> It is one of the most hopeful traits of the Gaelic revival that whilst promoting the study of the language and literature of the country it also provides a certain amount of harmless amusement which has a tendency to lessen the dullness that is so much deplored in Irish life, and to which some of the greatest thinkers of the day attribute in some degree the deplorable tide of emigration that is constantly going on from our shores.[33]

For many, no doubt, the enjoyment of such "harmless amusement" was at least as attractive as learning a difficult language. Given the puritanical mentality of the Irish clergy, these opportunities for sociability between the sexes could be very disturbing indeed, and one of the more famous incidents of the League's early history revolved around the tirade of priestly scruples, youthful sociability, and local leadership provided by a returned emigrant in the face of clerical wrath.

Things began smoothly enough in August of 1905 when the Rory O'More Branch of the Gaelic League was started in Portarlington. Father E. O'Leary, the Parish Priest, provided his blessing, the use of the parish hall for meetings, and though he took no active interest in its affairs, he

accepted the presidency of the fledging branch. Such generosity, however, did not insure that the branch would
be conducted on lines completely acceptable to Father
O'Leary, and he soon was disturbed to learn that the League's evening classes were attended by enthusiasts of both
sexes. Father O'Leary's forthright response was to condemn
mixed classes and, with the diplomatic skill so characteristic
of Irish country priests, he insisted that the young women of
the neighborhood would find no attraction in language
classes, were it not for the fact that the streets of the town
were unlighted. The lay leaders of the branch, insensitive to
their Christian duty and unaware of their proper role in an
Irish country town, expelled their reverend president and
continued the mixed classes even though the parish hall soon
became unavailable for meetings. During a Sunday sermon
in which the curate was denouncing the branch and its
leadership, who happened to be present, the leaders—P. T.
MacGinley in particular—rose, denounced the curate in
kind, and left the church.

Such irreverence could not fail to be brought to the
attention of Bishop Foley of Kildare, who stood behind his
clergy and directed the offenders to sign a formal apology, a
draft of which had been prepared by Father O'Leary. When
they refused, Father O'Leary started another branch. The
Executive Committee (Coiste Gnotha) in Dublin, after
hearing from the Rory O'More Executive, decided that two
branches in the same parish were excessive, and refused to
affiliate Father O'Leary's. Now armed with conclusive
proof of the League's anticlericalism, the energetic priest set
about trying to reform it. In a circular letter to the Catholic
clergy, he informed them of the dangerous situation and
asked them "to use your influence with the branch or
branches of the League in your parish to insure the election
of a proper and reliable delegate to the Ard Fheis."[34] This
done, the fateful Árd Fheis met in August of 1906. Though

the turnout was large, with priests and women seemingly more numerous than usual, the delegates supported "Rory" overwhelmingly. The results of the Executive Committee election showed MacGinley with the highest number of votes, while Father O'Leary, also a candidate, was spared the burden of having to deal with anticlericals.[35]

"The Battle of Portarlington" is significant in many ways, not least because the matter did not end at the Árd Fheis. But for the purposes of this paper, it is necessary to make only a few points. First, in its local branches the Gaelic League could disturb the tranquility of the Irish countryside and raise challenges to clerical supremacy in the area of acceptable social mores. Second, the opposition to Father O'Leary was led by MacGinley and S. B. Roche, both of whom were civil servants who had spent time in other parts of the British Isles and neither of whom was then residing in his native place; this implies, among other things, that they had acculturated to more secular society. During the course of the dispute they were reported to their superiors, but their position as civil servants left them economically invulnerable to clerical sanctions. A third member of the Executive was less fortunate. Joseph MacManus, a young shop assistant, was dismissed from his position when he refused to sign the apology to Father O'Leary. After several months of unemployment he emigrated to New York.[36] Finally, MacGinley, Roche, and W. P. Ryan, who supported them vigorously, had no doubts that by their opposition to this particular instance of clerical arrogance, they were contributing to the regeneration of Ireland. Though the nationalization of Irish agriculture, which linked rural Ireland to pasturage, emigration, and the British market, seemed to their nostalgic emigrant eyes to be indicative of the devitalization they wished to arrest, they also saw with eyes that had grown accustomed to a more modern, secular environment. From that perspective Ireland remained a very backward and excessively deferential society. Their years abroad provided them with an expanded sense of possibility, and it was difficult for them to accept the notion that the established order in Irish country towns represented an unalloyed manifestation of divine wisdom. Though all were Catholics, they also defined their loyalties in terms of the secular and abstract ideals of the nation and its culture. Portarlington only marked the beginnings of their difficulties with the Catholic clergy, and it is unnecessary to claim exclusive importance or centrality in the development of Irish cultural nationalism for them to appreciate that they were not without impact. Indeed, though they considered themselves outsiders in Britain and passionately identified themselves with Ireland, they were also men of the periphery in their native land.

While recent work has laid more stress on the positive contributions of activist British civil servants than has been usual heretofore, there is no argument that Ireland underwent a major social transformation in the course of the nineteenth-century.[37] Nor is there much disagreement about the extraordinarily important role of emigration in Irish history. But the relationship of these developments to the growth of national consciousness has received very little attention.[38] Practically no attention has been given to the impact of those who emigrated and—partly as a result of being "marginal men" in a strange environment—returned with a heightened national consciousness. The evidence presented in connection with the Gaelic League, though hardly definitive, indicates that it was significant. The peasants and emigrants had a critical impact on Ireland at the turn of the century, and the socio-political scene was greatly altered by the Gaelic League in the quarter century prior to 1916.

[1]*Oxford English Dictionary* (Oxford, England: Clarendon Press, 1961), Volume VII.

[2]David Riesman, *The Lonely Crowd* (New Haven: Yale University Press, 1950), Chapter 1.

[3]C. von Dietze, "Peasantry," *Encyclopedia of the Social Sciences,* Edwin R. A. Seligman, ed. (New York: Macmillan, 1934), XII, 48-52.

[4]The figures used here are derived from the excellent chapter on "The Economic Environment" in F. S. L. Lyons, *Ireland Since the Famine* (London: Weindenfeld and Nicolson, 1971), pp. 22-58. The figures, particularly the early ones, are approximate. They are derived from different sources, and depending on how they are computed, the total number of holdings ranges from 758,000 to 814,000.

[5]Ibid., p. 42. Though the typical farm was still less than thirty acres, most of the actual land was occupied by farms of more than thirty acres.

[6]Minute Book of the Executive Committee of the Gaelic League (M. B. hereafter), July 7, 1897 - Dec. 21, 1898. MS. 9799, National Library of Ireland.

[7]*Irish Peasant*, May 5, 1906. Under "Irish Pioneers."

[8]Ibid., Sept. 15, 1906.

[9]Giovanni Costigan, *A History of Modern Ireland, with a Sketch of Earlier Times* (New York: Pegasus, 1969), p. 260.

[10]M. B., Jan. 4, 1899 - May 27, 1902. MD 9800, N.L.O., passim.

[11]P. S. O'Hegarty, *A History of Ireland Under the Union* (London: Methuen, 1952), p. 606. See also Edmund Curtis, *A History of Ireland* (New York: Van Nostrand, 1937), pp. 380-81; Donal McCartney, "From Parnell to Pearse (1891-1921)," *The Course of Irish History*, T. W. Moody and F. X. Martin, eds. (New York: Weybright and Talley, 1967), p. 294; Costigan, op. cit., p. 260.

[12]John Redmond, "The Present Position of the Irish Question," *Forum,* XXIX (June, 1900), 397-400.

[13]Wilfred Scawen Blunt, *My Diaries* (New York: Alfred A. Knopf, 1921), II, 20.

[14]T. P. O'Connor, *Memoirs of an Old Parliamentarian* (London: Ernest Benn, 1929), II, 50-53.

[15]Hyde delivered the speech on November 25, 1892. It was printed in *The Revival of Irish Literature* (London: Fisher Unwin, 1894), which also contained addresses by Charles Gavan Duffy and George Sigerson.

[16]See Donald H. Akenson, *The Irish Education Experiment* (London and Toronto: Routledge and Kegan Paul and University of Toronto Press, 1970), pp. 376-385.

[17]W. B. Yeats, *The Autobiography of William Butler Yeats* (New York: Macmillan, 1969), pp. 124.

[18]See D. P. Moran, "Politics, Nationality, and Snobs," *New Ireland Review,* XII (November, 1899), 132-136 for a devastating commentary on these popular journals.

[19]Thomas N. Brown, "Nationalism and the Irish Peasant, 1800-1848," *Review of Politics*, XV (October, 1953), 403-445.

[20]Emmet Larkin has argued recently that these "graces" became widely diffused only in the third quarter of the nineteenth century. See "The Devotional Revolution in Ireland, 1850-1875," *American Historical Review*, LXXVII (June, 1972), 625-652.

[21]See Oscar Handlin, *The Uprooted* (Boston: Little Brown, 1952), Chapter 7, for a general consideration of this phenomenon. A particularly interesting illustration from the London-Irish point of view can be found in W. P. Ryan, *The Irish Literary Revival* (London: The Author, 1894), Chapter 2. Also see L. Perry Curtis, *Anglo-Saxons and Celts* (University of Bridgeport, Connecticut: Conference on British Studies, 1968) and *Apes and Angels* (Washington: Smithsonian Institution Press, 1971).

[22]*An Claidheamh Soluis*, Sept. 26, 1903. See also the *Irish Peasant*, April 7, 1906, where the spirit of the Gaelic League of London is described: "In the League were dozens of folk ordinarily in revolt against the whole trend of life around them. In the League they were at home, they were themselves upholding an unpopular standard in a strange land and they seemed necessarily more intense in their faith, more zealous in their work than the folk in Ireland at home would be."

[23]D. P. Moran, "Is the Irish Nation Dying?", *New Ireland Review*, X (Dec., 1898), 208-214.

[24]Lyons, op. cit., pp. 3-92, 219-242.

[25]W. P. Ryan, *The Pope's Green Island*, (London: James Nisbet, 1912), pp. 2 and 6.

[26]For a detailed account of this episode see my dissertation "W. P. Ryan and the Irish-Ireland Movement," (University of Connecticut: 1970), pp. 163-214.

[27]Among the non-Irish-Irelanders were D. J. O'Donoghue, (March 24, 1906), Dr. George Sigerson (April 14, 1906), Standish O'Grady (May 19, 1906), P. J. McCall (July 14, 1906), R. Barry O'Brien (July 21, 1906), and W. B. Yeats (Sept. 8, 1906).

[28]These were Douglas Hyde, Ernest Joynt, and J. O. Hannay; Dr. John P. Henry and T. O'Neill Russell are other possibilities.

[29]See *Irish Peasant*, May 26, 1906, for a reference to D. P. Moran's article "One Hundred Years of Irish Humbug," which was an attack on Anglo-Irish literature in general and the Irish Literary Society of London in particular. Ryan's view was similar to Moran's, if less caustic. He remarked that "the [Anglo] Irish literary movement, starting from the Irish Literary Society [London] and the National Literary Society [Dublin] did not reach the masses at all." See Ryan's unpublished reminiscences "Quests and Companions," p. 221 in the possession of Mrs. Sarah E. Ryan.

[30]Ibid., Dec. 30, 1905, and March 5 and June 30, 1906.

[31]Ibid., June 30, 1906.

[32]Conor Cruise O'Brien, ed., *The Making of Modern Ireland* (University of Toronto Press, 1960).

³³*Irish Peasant*, Sept. 3, 1905.

³⁴Ibid., July 7, 1906.

³⁵For a detailed account of the proceedings see ibid., Aug. 18, 1906. See also W. P. Ryan, *The Pope's Green Island*, pp. 102-115.

³⁶Ibid., May 12, 1906.

³⁷Lyons, op. cit., Akenson, op. cit., Oliver MacDonaugh, *Ireland* (Englewood Cliffs, New Jersey: Prentice Hall, 1968), Edward Norman, *A History of Modern Ireland* (Coral Gables: University of Miami Press, 1971).

³⁸The outstanding exception is Thomas N. Brown, *Irish American Nationalism* (Philadelphia: Lippincott, 1966).

JOHN UNTERECKER

# Countryman, Peasant and Servant in the Poetry of W. B. Yeats

ONE OF THE THINGS I shall hope to find when a "definitive" biography of Yeats finally comes along is an accurate picture of what life was like in the kitchens, stableyards, and barns of Rosses Point and Sligo. For it is in these places, Yeats hints, that much of his character was shaped.

I look forward to finding out who the stableboy was who, Yeats says in his autobiography, was his closest companion, the boy with whom Yeats climbed Ben Bulben's side in search of trout pools, who helped Yeats dig for the earthworms with which they baited their fishhooks, who shared with Yeats in a hayloft a book of political poems, Yeats's first experience, he tells us, of "the pleasure of rhyme." Except for a few sentences in "Reveries over Childhood and Youth" and—just possibly—references in three

John Unterecker, a noted Yeats scholar, is Professor of English at Columbia University. He is perhaps best known for his *Reader's Guide to W. B. Yeats*, though he has written excellent biographical-critical studies of Hart Crane and Lawrence Durrell.

This paper is based on informal remarks made during the conference on "The Irish Peasant: 1800-1916." The author is grateful to Dan Casey for an opportunity to listen to tapes of the meeting and for his assistance in preparing a rough transcript—which has been vastly departed from. Quotations are from the "Reveries" section of *Autobiographies*, from the *Collected Poems*, and from the 1903 dedication of *Cathleen ni Houlihan* that is reprinted in the notes to the first edition of *Plays for an Irish Theatre* (1911).

crucial poems, that boy, Yeats's "principal friend" of childhood, has vanished. And with him, of course, has vanished
an entire formative world: the rich, secret, compulsive
world of childhood and adolescence that no autobiogra-
pher, no matter how candid, can ever quite reconstruct. Yet
somewhere—in letters unpublished or perhaps undiscover-
ed—the key to those barns, stables, and kitchens may,
casually unnoticed, be waiting for the man with insight
enough to restore the past and recover for us not just the
general nature of a child's world but the real persons—
persons with names, and homes, and private histories—who
moved through it. How much more, I think, we might know
of Yeats if we could see him through the eyes of that
stableboy, for they had shared life early; surely it is out of a
poet's shared life that everything else must flow.

I look forward also to learning more, much more, about
the Middletons, who "let their houses decay and the glass fall
from the windows of their greenhouses," but who were
sometimes gifted with second sight. They lacked pride and
reserve, Yeats notes, and "took the nearest for friends and
were always in and out of the cottages of pilots and tenants."
"Certainly the first faery stories that I heard," he goes on,
"were in the cottages about their houses." How much more,
again, would we learn of the reality of Yeats's childhood
could we have access to the memories of those Middletons
and their cottagers.

But what we need is what we cannot have: the casual
words, the tone of the life, the ghost stories not as Yeats
recollects them in *The Celtic Twilight* but as they were
spoken on late summer evenings, Ben Bulben and Knock-
narea already swallowed up in darkness, the long summer
twilight lengthening out over the Rosses and beyond them
over the Atlantic. The Middletons Yeats knew in his childhood, their tenants so full of ghost stories, the boy who
introduced Yeats first to poetry, riding, and fishing are now
long since dead and buried, their voices at best ghostly

memories badly imitated by living men and women. The past is gone.

• • • • • •

The past is gone, and we are sadly misled if we try to reconstruct it in terms of the present. For we have moved far away—especially in America, but in Ireland as well—from the world of *inhabited* kitchens, stables, and barns. What we have instead are single-family houses with two-car garages or, in cities, compact air-conditioned apartments with all-electric kitchens. The young poet growing up in America has no real access to a servant class, much less a peasantry in tenant cottages. The ghost stories he hears are on television.

I labor this point, because we sometimes fail to visualize accurately what Yeats and most of his contemporaries took for granted. Almost every child of Yeats's class—upper-middle in behavior and lower-middle in income—grew up with a double family: the one he ate meals with and the other one that much of his time he lived with. And more often than not it was with this latter, informal "family" of servants and neighboring cottagers that he shared his emotional and imaginative life.

• • • • • •

Certainly this double life characterized the girlhood of Yeats's friend Maud Gonne, who, raised in a British army officer's family by an Irish servant girl and a frail mother, found herself—especially after her mother's death—growing increasingly contemptuous of her assorted English aunts and uncles. The servant girl's nationalism became Maud Gonne's own when Maud discovered that the dashing young father she admired more than any other person intended to leave the British army and devote himself to Irish nationalistic causes. His sudden death when Maud was still in her teens and the servant girl's stories of peasant suffering in the west of Ireland conjoined to turn a beautiful young girl into a passionate political activist. Maud Gonne's "family" became an amalgam of the servant's background and her father's soldierly idealism.

What Yeats and Maud Gonne shared in being brought up half by servants whose backgrounds were in the peasantry and half by well educated, sophisticated men was a kind of double family life. But a very similar pattern had developed in the peasantry itself. For all across famine-ridden rural nineteenth-century Ireland an informal system of foster parentage had sprung up. When starving parents found it impossible to raise their own children, they passed those children on to more prosperous neighbors. Such children grew up literally with two families. Though sociologists like to point out the stresses this led to when parent and foster parent clashed, there were also distinct advantages to a fosterage system. When "family" included at least two family units, affection of one kind or another was almost always available to children.

What Yeats experienced—climbing the mountain with a stableboy, talking to peasant girls and sailors' wives in his mother's kitchen, talking to second-sighted Mary Battle in the kitchen of his uncle George Pollexfen—was of course not fosterage, but there was an overlap of affection that reminds one of it. Perhaps a nearer analogy can be found in the deep south of nineteenth-century America. One thinks immediately of William Faulkner, who was brought up by Callie Barr, the warm, generous "mammy" who became the model for Dilsey in his novels. The mother who bore him was white; the "mammy" who raised him was black. He honored both women. But the woman who suckled him and who saw him through the traumas of childhood was Callie; and when she died at the age of one hundred and three, he saw to it that her funeral was performed in his front parlor. Faulkner himself gave a brief funeral oration and then read aloud

passages from *The Sound and the Fury,* breaking into tears
when he came to the words he had years before written
about Dilsey. Where living is shared, a child brought up by
two mothers, love is almost inevitably shared. The doubled
family life that results is richer and more complex than the
simple hygenic one present-day Americans have evolved.

To locate another analogy in Faulkner, we have only to
consider the interrelationship of feeling between Chick
Mallison in all of the stories that touch on him and Aleck
Sander, the son of the Mallison family's black servants. What
Chick discovers in Aleck is a brotherhood deeper than kin or
skin. For as well as each other's companionship, they share a
sense of each other's differences: the black servant world
that Chick can enter only via Aleck, and for Aleck, the
closed white world that disintegrates under the pressure of
Chick's casual yet deep-rooted affection.

● ● ● ● ● ●

Now, perhaps, we can turn to Yeats's own fisherman—
not, this time, to the stableboy who climbed Ben Bulben
with Yeats, the two of them getting up before dawn to ride
or perhaps even to walk the five miles to Drumcliff, but
rather to a fisherman who "does not exist," who is "but a
dream."

● ● ● ● ● ●

This imaginary fisherman comes into being not long
after Yeats's fiftieth birthday. Within the poem "The Fisherman," Yeats credits him as being invented a year or so
earlier. But there is, I believe, no doubt at all that he is
modelled on the typical countryman of Yeats's childhood,
the sort of man his brother would later paint from memories
of Sligo, the kind of man Yeats heard of in the quasi-
fosterage of family kitchens and neighboring cottages, the
rough, wild, wise man with so little to lose that he is

literally free—under no spiritual or contractual bondage to any man or even to any nation.

Though we later learn Yeats's fisherman is imaginary, Yeats begins his poem by insisting on his reality:

> Although I can see him still,
> The freckled man who goes
> To a grey place on a hill
> In grey Connemara clothes
> At dawn to cast his flies,
> It's long since I began
> To call up to the eyes
> This wise and simple man.

He symbolizes, Yeats suggests, that Irish audience Yeats had always hoped to reach—the audience who so far had found a tongue only in the oral tradition. Here, Yeats says, is the man of his "own race" for whom all of Yeats's work had been intended. But immediately "the reality" of modern Dublin stares him in the face: the corrupt middle-class with its ill-gotten wealth clutched tight; "craven," "insolent" men whom Yeats hates; "witty," "clever" men who have sold themselves to the mob and who are responsible for

> The beating down of the wise
> And great Art beaten down.

To invent such a fisherman as he has already described, Yeats concludes, will be a way to repudiate that self-centered, self-serving mob who dominate modern life:

> Maybe a twelvemonth since
> Suddenly I began,
> In scorn of this audience,
> Imagining a man,

And his sun-freckled face,
And grey Connemara cloth,
Climbing up to a place
Where stone is dark under froth,
And the down-turn of his wrist
When the flies drop in the stream;
A man who does not exist,
A man who is but a dream;
And cried, 'Before I am old
I shall have written him one
Poem maybe as cold
And passionate as the dawn.'

Readers acquainted with all of Yeats's work will probably recognize a familiar likeness in this fisherman. He reminds one a little of Cuchulain, a little of Red Hanrahan, and
he anticipates a whole crowd of honest, plainspoken men
who show up over and over in the work of Yeats's last fifteen
years. He's a peasant figure, a countryman—no doubt of
that—but he's a peasant figure with a difference: a peasant
figure assigned Yeats's mature sensibility. It's as if Yeats and
his boyhood friend had, growing up, amalgamated—turned
into one figure—an idealized poet-peasant totally different
from the romanticized peasantry a much younger Yeats had
presented in *The Celtic Twilight*. Far too many of those
peasants, Yeats came to realize, were sentimentalized. As
early as 1903, in dedicating *Cathleen ni Houlihan* to Lady
Gregory, Yeats despaired of ever accurately reproducing
the language of the true countryman:

> When I was a boy I used to wander about at Rosses
> Point and Ballisodare listening to old songs and stories. I
> wrote down what I heard and made poems out of the
> stories or put them into the little chapters of the first
> edition of *The Celtic Twilight*, and that is how I began
> to write in the Irish way.

Then I went to London to make my living, and though I spent a part of every year in Ireland and tried to keep the old life in my memory by reading every country tale I could find in books or old newspapers, I began to forget the true countenance of country life. . . . Then you brought me with you to see your friends in the cottages, and to talk to old wise men on Slieve Echtge . . . . You taught me to understand again, and much more perfectly than before, the true countenance of country life. . . . but I could not get down out of that high window of dramatic verse, and in spite of all you had done for me I had not the country speech.

By 1915, when he was working on "The Fisherman," Yeats had long since given up the hope of imitating country speech; what he now saw as more important was to recover the truth of country attitudes. His fisherman would not have to sound like a peasant if he could be emblematic of peasant wisdom. And so what the fisherman demands of Yeats, when he finally appears, is not a poetry that "sounds like" a countryman but rather a poetry that is faithful to the countryman's tough, uncompromising perception of the world. This new "wise" peasant demands a poetry that is antisentimental, a poetry that is simultaneously earthy and honest— "cold," in Yeats's terms, and "passionate."

In 1916 fisherman and the "one" poem that Yeats had promised him were, however, put aside for a number of years. Instead, Yeats worked on dance plays and worked out the system that culminated in *A Vision*, almost as a by-product producing that great body of poetry that was to give him an international reputation. The fisherman was, however, never forgotten and, a dozen years after his first appearance, he spectacularly reappears—this time in "The Tower," where he is chosen to inherit Yeats's faith and pride.

At the beginning of that poem he is, Yeats asserts, no

longer in any way separated from Yeats. He is indeed what
Yeats had once been: a boy climbing Ben Bulben's back. But
he is in disguise. The corrupting force of age has superim-
posed the wrecked body of the old writer on that of the
virile young man.

> What shall I do with this absurdity—
> O heart, O troubled heart—this caricature,
> Decrepit age that has been tied to me
> As a dog's tail?
>                    Never had I more
> Excited, passionate, fantastical
> Imagination, nor an ear and eye
> That more expected the impossible—
> No, not in boyhood when with rod and fly,
> Or the humbler worm, I climbed Ben Bulben's back
> And had the livelong summer day to spend.

Abruptly, however, the poem shifts its focus. Pacing on the
battlements of his tower, Yeats broods upon old age and
upon the "meaning" of life. That meaning, he decides, must
somewhere be found: perhaps in the peasantry, perhaps in
the servant class, perhaps among the poets, perhaps in the
aristocracy . . . and he proceeds to call up "images and
memories" from the landscape about him: aristocratic Mrs.
French and a faithful servant who, divining her wish, clip-
ped an insolent farmer's ears; a peasant girl whose praises
had been sung by the wandering poet Raftery; a figure from
Yeats's own short stories, Hanrahan; an ancient, bankrupt
master of the tower itself. To all of these figures, Yeats
would put the same question:

> Did all old men and women, rich and poor,
> Who trod upon these rocks or passed this door,
> Whether in public or in secret rage
> As I do now against old age?

The answer is in their eyes, and he dismisses all of them
except Hanrahan, the "old lecher with a love on every wind"
whom he had created when he himself was a young man,
Hanrahan, who, wise in country ways and independent
enough to stand up to peasant or aristocrat, bears a speaking
likeness to the fisherman Yeats so much needs and admires.
The question for him is a far more personal one than Yeats
had put to his other assembled ghosts; for Hanrahan, like
Cuchulain, is a man of action, Yeats's opposite, his Mask,
and so what Yeats must most strive to become. Yeats asks
him a question about love: Does one's imagination dwell the
most upon a woman won or lost? Yeats gives Hanrahan no
opportunity to answer, but rather rushes on—assuming an
answer—to a passionate imperative: If on the lost, then
admit that you gave up pursuit of that woman because of
pride, cowardice, or conscience; and admit as well that
whenever the memory of her returns "the sun's/Under
eclipse and the day blotted out."

   With Hanrahan in front of his mind's eye, it seems for a
moment that Yeats has forgotten the fisherman. But Hanrahan is the fisherman's surrogate. There is no transition at all
to the next section of the poem:

> It is time that I wrote my will;
> I choose upstanding men
> That climb the streams until
> The fountain leap, and at dawn
> Drop their cast at the side
> Of dripping stone. . . .

To such men, Yeats says, he will leave everything that really
matters; his pride and his faith. His pride is

> The pride of people that were
> Bound neither to Cause nor to State,

> Neither to slaves that were spat on,
> Nor to the tyrants that spat. . . .

His faith is faith in the integrity of man; for man, Yeats says—in contradiction to much that he himself had at one time or another earlier asserted—invented the idea of Heaven. Having invented a Heaven, man promptly created the arts and drew on love in order to mirror that Heaven. Out of the stuff of earth, lovers and artists make "a superhuman/ Mirror-resembling dream."

But both lovers and artists need a model for excellence. And it is as this model that the fisherman is invoked. Yeats's legacy is therefore far from capricious. The fisherman— now become the hope of mankind—will inherit Yeats's pride and his faith. The "cold" and "passionate" poem Yeats had a dozen years earlier promised to write has at last been produced:

> I leave both faith and pride
> To young upstanding men
> Climbing the mountain-side,
> That under the bursting dawn
> They may drop a fly;
> Being of that metal made
> Till it was broken by
> This sedentary trade.

Yeats was sixty-two when he wrote "The Tower." Ten years later—within two years of his death—he turned again toward the "deep-rooted things" that he most valued. Again he tackled a poem full of death and celebration, a poem that is cold—that forbids weeping—and that is shot through with passionate conviction. "John Synge, I and Augusta Gregory," he says in "The Municipal Gallery Revisited,"

All that we did, all that we said or sang
Must come from contact with the soil, from that
Contact everything Antaeus-like grew strong.
We three alone in modern times had brought
Everything down to that sole test again,
Dream of the noble and the beggar-man.

• • • • • •

Yeats and his friend the stableboy, rising before dawn, had walked the back roads between Rosses Point and the steep sides of Ben Bulben, or had saddled up their horses and ridden the five miles or so of country roads, or most likely of all had galloped bareback across stony fields. However they got to the mountain, they had no choice but to pass the ancient Celtic cross that one of Yeats's ancestors had been responsible for restoring or the church and churchyard down the road from it that a Yeats had once presided over. They would have passed the broken round tower across the road from churchyard and cross and gone a mile or so to the base of the mountain, tethered horses if they had ridden the distance that was really too long for even an ambitious boy's hike, unpacked their fishing gear, and climbed to the high pools where trout, they knew, lay waiting.

• • • • • •

Four months before his death, Yeats wrote the poem that was intended to appear at the beginning of his final collection and that now is conventionally printed last in all editions of Yeats's collected poems. Like most of the poetry of his old age, "Under Ben Bulben" combines cold imperatives with passionate conviction. In the penultimate section he returns to that "dream of the noble and the beggar-man" that had informed "The Municipal Gallery Revisited," but this time Yeats generalizes. His concern is that all members

of "the peasantry" and all "hardriding country gentlemen"
be commemorated in the poetry of the future.

> Irish poets, learn your trade,
> Sing whatever is well made,
> Scorn the sort now growing up
> All out of shape from toe to top,
> Their unremembering hearts and heads
> Base-born products of base beds.
> Sing the peasantry, and then
> Hard-riding country gentlemen,
> The holiness of monks, and after
> Porter-drinkers' randy laughter;
> Sing the lords and ladies gay
> That were beaten into the clay
> Through seven heroic centuries;
> Cast your mind on other days
> That we in coming days may be
> Still the indomitable Irishry.

The poem ends where it begins: at Yeats's gravesite.
The final imperative, Yeats's epitaph, demands of us that
coldness Yeats has successfully driven himself to. Whoever
we are—hard-riding country gentleman, hard-riding stableboy, hard-riding child in pursuit of a dream still too large to
be conceived—our subject, the only one worth having, is the
totality of being, transient, perpetually dying, perpetually
renewed:

> Under bare Ben Bulben's head
> In Drumcliff churchyard Yeats is laid.
> An ancestor was rector there
> Long years ago, a church stands near,
> By the road an ancient cross.
> No marble, no conventional phrase;

On limestone quarried near the spot
By his command these words are cut:

> *Cast a cold eye*
> *On life, on death.*
> *Horseman, pass by!*

• • • • • •

On an August evening of 1973, I stood in a crowded room talking to John McMorrow. We were not talking of Yeats but of Sligo itself. A cool evening wrapped the city in misty rain. John told me how much the town had meant to him, the countryside: river and mountains and sea. It was a world, he said, worth growing old in. Then I did ask him about Yeats. Had he ever known him? Not really, but a long time ago he had met a man who knew him well. "Who was that?" "Mickey Gilligan, a great old man who used to live at Drumcliff, a great fisherman in his time." "Had Gilligan ever gone fishing with Yeats?" I asked. "The very question I asked him. Of course, all of this was a long time ago—when we were talking—over in Drumcliff. But I remember his answer exactly. 'I taught Willie Yeats everything he knew about fishing,' Mickey Gilligan told me. 'I taught Willie Yeats everything he knew about fishing—and a damned poor fisherman he was, too!'" I hadn't the wit, I was so startled, to ask John McMorrow if Mickey Gilligan had ever been a stable-boy for a Yeats or a Pollexfen or a Middleton. Chances are, of course, that he hadn't been.

# Jack B. Yeats's Picture
# of the Peasant

IN 1887, JACK B. YEATS left Sligo, where his grandparents had reared him since infancy, and joined his family in London. (He was in fact born in London in 1871, but straitened family circumstances forced a West Ireland rearing.) Living henceforth in London, Devon, and Dublin, he was never to make his home there again. Yet in his painting he was to return there, in a sense even live there, in the living past of his youth. The title of a water color of 1900 is a synechdoche for much of his work: "Memory Harbor." The customs and environs of turn-of-the-century Sligo he knew well, and he knew all the types, stylized and universalized, who gathered there.

Sometimes these were the countryfolk who came in for the races. But the humble folk who really imposed upon his artistic consciousness were either small-town or urban or marginal (e.g., sailors, jockeys, carnival artists, tinkers). At first, it may seem anomalous that a painter who glorified Irish landscape and usually placed man and nature in provocative juxtaposition painted so few people who can be unmistakably identified as part of the peasantry. Indeed, it would seem that he interacted with them less than did his brother, who went among them first as an impressionable

Marilyn Gaddis Rose is best known in Anglo-Irish studies for her research on Jack B. Yeats. She is Professor and Chairman of Comparative Literature at State University of New York at Binghamton.

child and later as a folklorist. Of course, he must have talked to them, though he did not study Irish until after his marriage in 1894. He saw them pass by, and he mingled with them, but always as the outsider, always as an observer. He was not given to speculation on class structure like his brother, and he evidently did not identify with the peasantry. He incorporated sailor, jockey, circus entertainer, and tinker into his own consciousness; they figured in his fantasy life and were stored away in his memory pool. For the peasant, he was a kindly reporter, a sympathetic journalist-illustrator, when called upon.

When he observed the peasantry he did so with care. But when painting independently, he represented them, as he did the rest of us, as part of everyman. Because he did most of his work as an illustrator early in his career, most of the examples of his peasant portrayal use his early styles. In the corpus of his work such pictures are of already proven significance, for they show his explorations of the medium.[1] As social and intellectual documents, they are informative because of their demonstrated accuracy. As documents of personal and class psychology, they are quite intriguing, as is his relative neglect of the peasantry as a subject throughout his career. They are a subtle manifestation of the distancing of an Ascendancy artist toward a major supporting class of "mere" Irish. These early styles can, in fact, be analyzed as a modification of turn-of-the-century American cartoon draftsmanship and a simplification of the Art Nouveau emphatic line and decorative design. Such styles are highly suitable for illustrations that served the purpose now served by photography. But such techniques would never convey (or rarely convey) a deep involvement of the artist with his subject matter; he is held in check both by the conventions of the style and by the discipline of representational accuracy. (When an artist wants to visualize his commitment, he inevitably becomes Expressionistic, as the work of Yeats's continental contemporaries Munch, Barlach, and Grosz demonstrates.)

To remark that Yeats distanced himself from the peasant as a journalistic subject and later made incidental use of him as an artistic subject is not to disparage his social awareness and sympathy in any way. Where his journalistic illustrating is concerned, such distancing bespeaks a kindly editorializing. The fact is he did not single out unappealing characteristics, although his gallantry, courtesy, and moderation were surely offended by some of the features of rural life at the turn-of-the-century. He did not romanticize the farm laborer, although always prone to beautify what he found appealing, e.g., women, children, horses. He certainly did not exploit him for propagandistic ends. His figures are not pitiful. He was accurate and respectful, disposing the peasant as subject so that the viewer, also, will be encouraged to regard the subject with respect. His farmers and farm women are not, like his jockeys and tinkers, larger-than-life, they are people. And this is probably the fairest, most effective way he could depict them.

Although Yeats's nearly annual exhibitions from 1899-1925 usually had a title like "Sketches of Life in the West of Ireland," they did not dwell on the farm family of the period at work, worship, and play. They tended to show events, scenes, and personalities of the Port of Memory Harbor. The only pictures for which we can be sure that Yeats actually used the rural folk in his immediate purview are those which he did in collaboration with J. M. Synge. This collaboration was a response to a *Manchester Guardian* assignment in 1905-1906. The results were incorporated later in *In Wicklow, West Kerry and Connemara* (1911) and *The Aran Islands* (1907). In *The Aran Islands* Yeats worked both from his own observation and from Synge's photographs. (As for the hand-colored prints which he did for Cuala Press during these years, when they show a peasant type [and few of them do], they make him part of an Art Nouveau design. Aside from

following the conventions of the Irish craft revival, these
designs are not distinctively Irish. For example, "The Side-
Car" looks like a pseudo-medieval depiction of Phaeton's
chariot. The monk in the "Rune of Hospitality" could just as
well be climbing the Alps.)

As years went by, Yeats did less and less commissioned
illustrating. And, as has been well established by now, when
painting for himself, he painted his inner Ireland, peopled
by legend, kept in motion by the life cycle. Some exceptions
are quite effective. For example, "On Drumcliffe Strand"
(1918) shows sad faces of peasants watching Volunteers
instead of a horse race; "The Island Funeral" (1923) shows
humble mourners accompanying a splendid casket by boat;
"The Last Voyage" (1946) undoubtedly portrays the peasant
class; one of the three men is an Irish emigrant returning to
America.

To see how striking is the contrast between the peasant
as seen and the peasant as remembered, let us compare
"Man from Aranmore" (1905) and "Above the Fair" (1946).
In the water color painted the year of his collaboration with
Synge, the medium itself softens the contours of photo-
graphic composition, and the colors chosen, shades of violet
and gold, create an effect which even present-day camera
work could not achieve. However, the faintly blurred line
that results from water color pigment and the soft hues do
not make the rural islander a mythical composite. He is
merely a grand person snapped close-up and cropped. On
the other hand, in the oil painted the last decade of his life,
the remembered crowd of rural folk at a smalltown fair
could never have been so disposed (in the sense of placed or
arranged), colored, or illuminated. They are not only trans-
figured by the painter's inner vision, they seem to be part of
a transfiguring experience, and the overall pictorial effect
stimulates mythologizing in the viewer. Let us comment
upon each plate in more detail.

The islander poses at pier side. If we simplify down to

*On Drumcliffe Strand,* by Jack B. Yeats

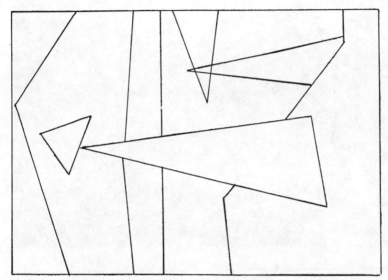

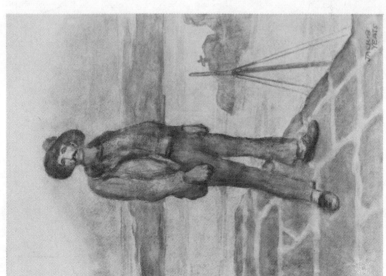

*The Man from Aranmore*, by Jack B. Yeats
Courtesy of the National Gallery of Ireland

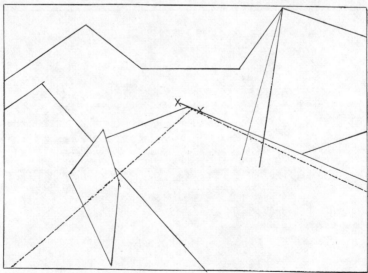

*Above the Fair,* by Jack B. Yeats

Courtesy of the National Gallery of Ireland

the geometric substructure here, we notice that the islander is an elongated scalene triangle in a vertical pattern of triangles: the pier, the boat mast, the cross and promontory at right midground, the background mountain. The pattern is kept from total regularity by having each triangle a little askew, a little off center, e.g., the mast, the cross, or by having askew triangles forming on the chief triangles, e.g., the islander's moustache, his hat. Another break in the regularity is caused by having two centers of interest. While the triangular lines tend to converge toward his chest, the natural point of interest is his face. This in turn has a shifting expression, i.e., his right eye indicates a glance off in his right-hand direction, while his left eye bears directly at us. The coloring creates additional diversion and movement of a very attentuated sort. The islander and the pier are in shades of violet, orchid, and lavender; his jacket has a tan overlay. The water of the inlet is dull gold, and upon the mountain at far left background is a dull orange spot. We are in the position of someone taking a photograph at a slightly lower elevation. Although the perspective is tilted upward, we do not receive an impression of distortion. The islander looms large before his native horizon but no more than he would in selective enlargement of a relatively conventional tourist snapshot. We have an elegantly washed picture of a man who stops just short of being a figure of romance.

Romance, however, almost in a chivalric sense, dominates "Above the Fair." Because of Yeats's palette knife and finger texture we do not receive this picture at a glance, as we did with "Man from Aranmore," a sketch designed in part at least to convey information. This painting, like those of Yeats's final period generally, is a pictorial equivalent of a poetic metaphor. This painting must emerge in our perception which must adjust itself to the painting before organizing its "content." When we do succeed finally in making the objects in "Above the Fair" stay in place, we are left with the usual mystification of Yeats's literary paintings. The disposi-

tion of space is Yeats's usual interacting triangles, here in a
pattern which is basically horizontal and which bears to our
left. The most dominant triangle is the magnificent white
horse in left foreground. Arranged behind it and its fair-
haired rider is a massive triangle of buildings and an adja-
cent triangle of crowd mingling dark and chalk faces. There
is a sharp upward vertical triangle building at upper right
which stands against a pale, nearly bare canvas of sky and a
dull green harbor. Only when the entire painting has been
staked down, so to speak, do we begin to pick out other
elusive features, i.e., the horses rounding up the crowd from
the rear and last of all, at least for me, the face of a splendid
red steed at right midground. Once the painting has revealed itself to us to this extent, we begin noticing a scene of
animation, real as well as painterly movement. Indeed,
instead of a painting which bears left to follow the white
horse whenever the parade resumes, we have an overlay
isosceles triangle going from the white horse to the black
and russet horses in the center of the painting to the red horse
on the right. The dark and chalk faces, like those of German
Expressionist Nolde, are pressed in among the four horses.
The artist, as the title indicates, is *above* the fair, yet if he
looks down into the glowering crowd, he must look up to the
white horse and its horseman, who gaze downward in the
artist's direction, more than they can be said to look at him.
The painting hints at an anecdote, at the approaching enact-
ment of some community ceremony. The sobriety of the
expressions promises a solemn rather than a carefree occasion. These are Irish rural folk of Yeats's Sligo youth, altered
in detail perhaps by his travelling days with Synge in his
young manhood, but they are figures of the imagination of a
painter who by artistic, creative choice does not show a real
county fair (although he undoubtedly saw many).

    What does this transformation of material mean? Most
obviously, these two pictures illustrate Yeats's changing,
maturing techniques; they show what happened when he

could use his talent solely for the expression of his inner vision. We could simply conclude that as he changed his technique, whatever he happened to be painting, be it a scene of peasant life or anything else, was modified accordingly.

This is the only premise which we can maintain with any certainty, but such a premise skirts the issue of Yeats's involvement with the farmer and farm laborer class of his youth and early manhood as material. As a beginning artist, a part-time journalist, he observed them; as a maturing artist he made sympathetic use of their pictorially narrative potential; as a well-established master he massed them in his mythical metaphors. But, when unrestricted in his use of material, he was not inclined to see people of this class very often. This is not to imply that he, to use a psychological term, factored rural folk out of his mental landscape (as he did, for example, the Catholic Church), and it certainly does not imply that he was not concerned about them as a fellow countryman. Once a scion of a small-town Ascendancy gentry, a boy who was a sailor, jockey, and circus entertainer in his heart, he painted the memory pool of his youth. When, in his early manhood, he observed the peasants more closely to make their way of life known to people of his own class, he was kind, careful, objective. The peasants were always there and he had good feelings toward them. But the land on which they made their living from 1800-1916 was his site of reverie; there he roamed for forty more years in the company of squireens, tinkers, and itinerant artists. Yeats and the peasantry lived in friendly juxtaposition, though they were worlds apart.

[1]For a discussion of these styles see Hilary Pyle, *Jack B. Yeats* (London:

Routledge and Kegan Paul, 1970) or my *Jack B. Yeats: Painter and Poet* (Berne: Herbert Lang, 1972).

## Acknowledgements

"The Man from Aranmore" and "Above the Fair" are reproduced with the courtesy of the National Gallery of Ireland; "On Drumcliffe Strand" is reproduced with the Courtesy of Miss Anne Butler Yeats and Mr. Michael Butler Yeats, holders of the copyright, and the National Gallery of Canada.

JOHN C. MESSENGER

# Bibliography

THE BIBLIOGRAPHY is a selected one and has been compiled over the past decade to serve students in my courses—Irish Folk Culture, Peasant Society and Culture, and Peasant Cultures: The Irish—at Indiana University and The Ohio State University. The titles were selected because of their appropriateness for the topics covered in the three courses and because of their availability in the University libraries and my private collection (especially journals, unpublished manuscripts, M.A. theses, and Ph.D. dissertations). The following are the topics that I have addressed: peasant society, culture, and personality; ethnographic and folkloristic research in Ireland; Irish prehistory and history; the Irish peasant; the Irish peasant and models of peasantry (consensus, coercion, historical, human cost, subculture, etc.); forms of Irish folklore; the art of storytelling in Ireland; functions of folklore in Ireland (peasant society and developing nation); influence of Irish peasant culture on modern esthetics; use of folklore in reconstructing Irish prehistory, history, and peasant culture; diffusion of Irish peasant culture to the New World; and contemporary peasant problems.

John C. Messenger has written books and articles on the Irish peasant. His most recent study, *Inis Beag: Isle of Ireland,* has been the subject of controversy among Irish social scientists and folklorists. He is Professor of Anthropology at Ohio State University.

All of the works are written in English, as few of my students have had command of Irish, German, Swedish, etc. Most of the citations are from the social sciences, in particular anthropology (ethnography, ethnology, social anthropology, and linguistics), sociology, and social psychology (psychiatry as well); though there are numerous entries from the borderline disciplines of folklore, human geography, and history. There are in addition, a number of literary works that are extremely insightful, as well as life histories and novels composed by Blasket and Aran Islanders, some of which I have used as textbooks.

The focus of the bibliography is on twentieth-century writings, especially those done during the past four decades, when dependable social scientific (and humanistic) studies were first conducted among Irish peasants. Much of the scholarly and literary materials of the nineteenth century are suspect, because they were produced by unskilled and often biased observers.

### Selected Bibliography

Aalen, F. H. E. and Hugh Brody. *Gola: The Life and Last Days of an Island Community*. Cork: The Mercier Press, 1969.

Adams, G. Brendan. "Language and Man in Ireland." *Ulster Folklife*, 16 (1970), 140-71.

Anderson, Robert T. *Modern Europe: An Anthropological Perspective*. Pacific Palisades: Goodyear Publishing Company, 1973, pp. 81-8.

Arensberg, Conrad M. *The Irish Countryman*. Gloucester: Peter Smith, 1937.

Arensberg, Conrad M. and Solon T. Kimball. *Family and Community in Ireland*. Cambridge: Harvard University Press, 1968.

Bales, Robert F. "Attitudes Toward Drinking in Irish Culture." In *Society, Culture, and Drinking Patterns*, eds. David J. Pittman and Charles R. Snyder. New York: John Wiley & Sons, 1962.

Barrington, Jonah. *The Ireland of Sir Jonah Barrington: Selections from His Sketches*, ed. Hugh Staples. London: Peter Owen, 1968.

Bauman, Richard. "John Millington Synge and Irish Folklore." *Southern Folklore Quarterly*, 27 (1963), 267-79.

Bax, Mart. *Harpstrings and Confessions: An Anthropological Study of Politics in Rural Ireland*. Amsterdam: University of Amsterdam, 1973.

*Béaloideas*. 39-41 (1971-1973), 1-424 (Essays and Studies Presented to Professor Séamus O' Duilearga).

Bell, Sam Hanna. *Within Our Province*. Belfast: Blackstaff Press, 1972.

Blanshard, Paul. *The Irish and Catholic Power: An American Interpretation*. London: Derek Verschoyle, 1954.

Broderick, John. *The Waking of Willie Ryan*. London: Weidenfeld and Nicolson, 1965.

Brody, Hugh. *Inishkillane: Change and Decline in the West of Ireland*. London: Allen Lane, 1973.

Browne, C. R. "The Ethnography of Ballycroy." *Proceedings of the Royal Irish Academy*, 4 (1896-98), 74-111.

_____. "The Ethnography of Carna and Mweenish." *Proceedings of the Royal Irish Academy*, 6 (1900-02), 503-34.

_____. "The Ethnography of Clare Island and Inishturk." *Proceedings of the Royal Irish Academy*, 5 (1898-1900), 40-72.

_____. "The Ethnography of Garumna and Lettermullen." *Proceedings of the Royal Irish Academy*, 5 (1898-1900), 223-68.

_____. "The Ethnography of Inishbofin and Inisshark." *Proceedings of the Royal Irish Academy*, 3 (1893-96), 317-70.

_____. "The Ethnography of the Mullet, Inishkea Islands and Portacloy." *Proceedings of the Royal Irish Academy*, 3 (1893-96), 587-649.

Buchanan, Ronald H. "The Folklore of An Irish Townland." *Ulster Folklife*, 2 (1956), 43-55.

————. "Rural Change in an Irish Townland." *Advancement of Science*, 2 (1958), 291-300.

————. "Tradition and Change in Rural Ulster." *Folklife*, 3 (1965), 39-45.

Buchanan, Ronald H., Emyr Jones and Desmond McCourt (eds.). *Man and His Habitat: Essays Presented to Emyr Estyn Evans*. London: Routledge and Kegan Paul, 1971.

Burke, Oliver J. *The South Isles of Aran (County Galway)*. London: Kegan Paul, Trench & Co., 1887.

Byrne, Patrick F. *Witchcraft in Ireland*. Cork: The Mercier Press, 1967.

Carbery, Mary. *The Farm by Lough Gur*. London: Longmans, Greene & Co., 1937.

Carleton, William. *Traits and Stories of the Irish Peasantry*. 8 vols. Cork and Dublin: The Mercier Press, 1973-74.

Clarke, Austin. *Twice Round the Black Church*. London: Routledge & Kegan Paul, 1962.

Colgan, Nathaniel. "Witchcraft in the Aran Islands." *Journal of the Royal Society of Antiquaries of Ireland*, 5 (1895), 84-5.

Colum, Padraic (ed.). *A Treasury of Irish Folklore*. New York: Crown Publishers, Inc., 1962.

Connell, Kenneth. *Irish Peasant Society*. Oxford: Clarendon Press, 1968.

————. *The Population of Ireland, 1750-1845*. Oxford: Clarendon Press, 1950.

Corkery, Daniel. *The Fortunes of the Irish Language*. Cork: The Mercier Press, 1966.

————. *The Hidden Ireland*. Dublin: Gill and Son, 1967.

————. *A Munster Twilight*. Cork: The Mercier Press, 1963.

Cowell, Sydney R. "Introduction." *Ethnic Folkways Library*. Album No. P1002 (Songs of Aran), 1957.

Cresswell, Robert. *Une Communauté Rurale de l'Irlande*. Paris: Institut d'Ethnologie, 1968.

————. "A CA Review of *Une Cummunauté Rurale de l'Irlande*." *Current Anthropology*, 13 (1972), 479-97.

Cross, Eric. *The Tailor and Ansty*. Cork: The Mercier Press, 1970.

Cullen, L. M. (ed.). *The Formation of the Irish Economy*. Cork: The Mercier Press, 1969.

_____. *Life in Ireland.* London: B. T. Batsford Ltd., 1968.

Curtis, L. Perry, Jr. *Apes and Angels: The Irishman in Victorian Caricature.* Newton Abbot: David & Charles, 1971.

Dall, Ian. *Here Are Stones.* London: Desmond Harmsworth, 1931.

Dalton, George. "Peasants in Anthropology and History." *Current Anthropology,* 13 (1972), 385-415.

Danaher, Kevin. "Animal Droppings as Fuel." *Folklife,* 6 (1968), 117-20.

_____. *In Ireland Long Ago.* Cork: The Mercier Press, 1962.

_____. *Irish Country People.* Cork: The Mercier Press, 1966.

_____. *Gentle Places and Simple Things.* Cork: The Mercier Press, 1970.

_____. *The Pleasant Land of Ireland.* Cork: The Mercier Press, 1970.

_____. *The Year in Ireland.* Cork: The Mercier Press, 1972.

de Freine, Sean. *The Great Silence.* Dublin: Foilseachain Naisiunta Teoranta, 1965.

Delargy, James H. "The Gaelic Story-Teller." *Proceedings of the British Academy,* 31 (1945), 177-221.

Douglas, J. N. H. "Emigration and Irish Peasant Life." *Ulster Folklife,* 9 (1963), 9-19.

Dowling, P. J. *A History of Irish Education.* Cork: The Mercier Press, 1971.

Doyle, Colman. *The People of Ireland.* Cork: The Mercier Press, 1971.

Dunne, David. "Lose the Heart, Destroy the Head." *Journal of St. Mary's Hospital* (Castlebar), Feb. 1970, pp. 22-35.

Edwards, Owen Dudley (ed.). *Conor Cruise O'Brien Introduces Ireland.* London: Andre Deutsch, 1969.

_____. "Ireland." In *Celtic Nationalism,* eds. Owen Dudley Edwards, et al. London: Routledge & Kegan Paul, 1968, pp. 5-209.

Edwards, R. Dudley and T. Desmond Williams (eds.). *The Great Famine.* Dublin: Browne and Nolan Limited, 1956.

Elwood, J. H. "The Population of Rathlin Island." *Ulster Medical Journal,* 37 (1968), 64-70.

_____. "Tory Island, 1841-1964." *Irish Journal of Medical Science,* 1 (1968), 19-24 and 72-73.

Evans, E. Estyn. "The Ecology of Peasant Life in Western Eu-
    rope." In *Man's Role in Changing the Face of the Earth*, ed.
    W. L. Thomas, Jr. Chicago: The University of Chicago Press,
    1956, pp. 217-39.

————. *Irish Folk Ways*. London: Routledge & Kegan Paul, 1957.

————. *Irish Heritage*. Dundalk: Dundalgan Press, 1942.

————. *The Irishness of the Irish*. Belfast: The Irish Association,
    1968.

————. *Mourne Country*. Dundalk: Dundalgan Press, 1967.

————. *The Personality of Ireland: Habitat, Heritage, and Histo-
    ry*. Oxford: Oxford University Press, 1973.

Fitzpatrick, Joyce. "Drinking Among Young People in Ireland."
    *Social Studies*, 1 (1972), 51-60.

Fleming, John B. "Folklore, Fact and Fancy." *Irish Journal of
    Medical Science*, No. 326 (1953), 50-63.

Fleure, H. J. *A Natural History of Man in Britain*. London:
    Fontana, 1971.

————. "Peasants in Europe." *Geography*, 28 (1943), 55-61.

Fox, Robin. "Kinship and Land Tenure on Tory Island." *Ulster
    Folklife*, 12 (1966), 1-17.

————. "Multilingualism in Two Communities." *Man*, 3 (1968),
    456-64.

————. "The Structure of Personal Names on Tory Island." *Man*,
    192 (1963), 153-6.

————. "Tory Island." In *Problems of Smaller Territories*, ed. R.
    Benedict. London: Athlone Press, 1967, pp. 112-33.

————. "The Vanishing Gael." *New Society*, Oct., 1962, 17-19.

Frankenberg, Ronald. *Communities in Britain*. Baltimore: Pen-
    guin Books, Inc., 1966, pp. 25-44.

Freeman, T. W. *Ireland: A General and Regional Geography*.
    London: Methuen and Co., Ltd., 1972.

Friis, Henning. *Development of Social Research in Ireland*. Dub-
    lin: Institute of Public Administration, 1965.

Gahagan, Michael B. *The Aran Islands*. Thesis, Victoria University
    of Manchester, 1965.

Gailey, R. Alan. "Aspects of Change in a Rural Community."
    *Ulster Folklife*, 5 (1959), 27-34.

————. *Irish Folk Drama*. Cork: The Mercier Press, 1969.

_____. "Settlement and Population in the Aran Islands." *Irish Geography*, 4 (1959), 65-78.

Glad, Donald D. "Attitudes and Experiences of American-Jewish and American-Irish Male Youth as Related to Differences in Adult Roles of Inebriety." *Quarterly Journal of Studies on Alcohol*, 8 (1948), 406-72.

Goldschmidt, Walter and Evalyn M. Junkel. "The Structure of the Peasant Family." *American Anthropologist*, 73 (1971), 1058-76.

Gorham, Maurice. *Ireland from Old Photographs*. London: B. T. Batsford, Ltd., 1971.

Gorman, Michael (ed.). *Ireland by the Irish*. London: Galley Press Ltd., 1963.

Gray, Tony. *The Irish Answer*. London: Heinemann, 1966.

Greeley, Andrew. *That Most Distressful Nation: The Taming of the American Irish*. Chicago: Quadrangle Books, 1972.

Green, E. R. R. (ed.). *Essays in Scotch-Irish History*. London: Routledge & Kegan Paul, 1969.

Greene, David. *The Irish Language*. Dublin: At the Three Candles, 1966.

Gwynn, Aubrey. "Cromwell's Policy of Transportation, Part 1." *Studies*, Dec. 1930, pp. 607-23.

_____. "Cromwell's Policy of Transportation, Part 2." *Studies*, June 1931, pp. 291-305.

_____. "Documents Relating to the Irish in the West Indies." *Analecta Hibernica*, Oct. 1932, pp. 139-286.

_____. "Early Irish Emigration to the West Indies (1612-1643)." *Studies*, Sept. 1929, pp. 377-93.

_____. "The First Irish Priests in the New World." *Studies*, June, 1932, pp. 213-28.

_____. "Indentured Servants and Negro Slaves in Barbados (1642-1650)." *Studies*, June 1930, pp. 279-94.

Hackett, Earle and M. F. Folan. "The ABO and Rh Blood Groups of the Aran Islands." *Irish Journal of Medical Science*, No. 390 (1958), 247-61.

Haddon, Alfred C. and C. R. Browne. "The Ethnography of the Aran Islands." *Proceedings of the Royal Irish Academy*, 2 (1891-93), 788-829.

Hannan, Damian. "Kinship, Neighbourhood, and Social Change in Irish Rural Communities." *The Economic and Social Review*, 3 (1972).

————. *Rural Exodus*. London: Geoffrey Chapman, 1970.

————. "Status Inequalities Within Families in Relation to Their Structural Differences." *The Economic and Social Review*, 1 (1970), 167-84.

Hardiman, James. *The History of the Town and County of the Town of Galway From the Earliest Period to the Present Time 1820*. Galway: The Connacht Tribune Printing and Publishing Company, Ltd., 1958.

Harris, Rosemary L. *Prejudice and Tolerance in Ulster*. Manchester: Manchester University Press, 1972.

————. "The Selection of Leaders in Ballybeg, Northern Ireland." *The Sociological Review*, 9 (1961), 137-49.

————. *Social Relations and Attitudes in a N. Irish Rural Area*. Thesis, University of London, 1954.

Healy, James N. *The Death of an Irish Town*. Cork: The Mercier Press, 1968.

Hedderman, B. N. *Glimpses of My Life in Aran*. Bristol: John Wright & Sons, Ltd., 1917.

Heslinga, M. W. *The Irish Border as a Cultural Divide*. Assen: Van Gorcum & Comp. N.V., 1962.

Hill, Lord George. *Facts From Gweedore*. (A Facsimile Reprint of the Fifth Edition, 1887, With an Introduction by E. Estyn Evans.) Belfast: The Queen's University of Belfast Institute of Irish Studies, 1971.

Hooton, Ernest A. and C. Wesley Dupertius. *The Physical Anthropology of Ireland*. Cambridge: Harvard University Press, 1955.

Humphreys, Alexander J. "The Family in Ireland." In *Comparative Family Systems*, ed. M. F. Nimkoff. Boston: Houghton, Mifflin Company, 1965, pp. 232-58.

————. *New Dubliners*. New York: Fordham University Press, 1966.

Kane, Eileen. *An Analysis of the Cultural Factors Inimical to the Development of the Nationalist-Revivalistic Industrial Process of Rural Irish Gaeltachts*. Diss., University of Pittsburgh, 1968.

_____. "Man and Kin in Donegal: A Study of Kinship Functions in a Rural Irish Community and an Irish-American Community." *Ethnology*, 7 (1968), 245-58.

_____. "Rural Poverty." *Social Studies*, 1 (1972), 413-26.

Kavanagh, Patrick. *The Great Hunger*. London: MacGibbon and Kee, 1964.

_____. *Tarry Flynn*. London: MacGibbon and Kee, 1968.

Keane, John B. *Big Maggie*. Cork: The Mercier Press, 1969.

_____. *The Field*. Cork: The Mercier Press, 1966.

_____. *The Year of the Hiker*. Cork: The Mercier Press, 1963.

Kearns, Kevin C. "Resuscitation of the Irish Gaeltacht." *Geographical Review*, 64 (1974), 82-110.

Kennedy, Robert E., Jr. *The Irish: Emigration, Marriage, and Fertility*. Berkeley: University of California Press, 1973.

Kiely, Jerome. *Seven Year Island*. London: Geoffrey Chapman, 1969.

Klimm, L. E. "Inishmore: An Outpost Island." *Geographical Review*, 17 (1927), 387-96.

Lavin, Mary. *At Sallygap and Other Stories*. Boston: Little, Brown and Company, 1947.

Lee, Joseph. *The Modernisation of Irish Society 1848-1918*. Dublin: Gill and Macmillan, 1973.

Lees, Nora L. *Bogs and Blarney*. Dublin: The Talbot Press Ltd., 1936.

Leitch, Maurice. *Poor Lazarus*. London: Panther Books, 1970.

Leyton, Elliott. "Conscious Models and Dispute Regulations in an Ulster Village." *Man*, 1 (1966), 534-42.

_____. *The One Blood: Kinship and Class in an Irish Village*. St. Johns: Memorial University of Newfoundland (by University of Toronto Press), 1975.

_____. "Spheres of Inheritance in Aughnaboy." *American Anthropologist*, 72 (1970), 1378-88.

Lucey, Dennis I. F. and Donald R. Kaldor. *Rural Industrialization: The Impact of Industrialization on Two Communities in Western Ireland*. London: Geoffrey Chapman, 1969.

MacNaught, J. C. "The Aran Isles." *Transactions of the Gaelic Society of Iverness*, 35 (1929), 83-97.

MacNeill, Maire. *The Festival of Lughnasa*. London: Oxford University Press, 1962.

Mason, Thomas H. *The Islands of Ireland*. Cork: The Mercier
     Press, 1967.
McCarthy, Joe and the Editors of *Life. Ireland*. New York: Time
     Incorporated, 1964.
McCourt, Desmond and R. Alan Gailey (eds.). *Studies in Folklife
     Presented to Emyr Estyn Evans*. Cultra Manor: Ulster Folk
     Museum, 1970.
McDevitt, James J., Jr. *Social Conflict in the Irish Peasant Subcul-
     ture*. Thesis, The Ohio State University, 1972.
McDowell, R. B. (ed.). *Social Life in Ireland 1800-45*. Dublin: At
     the Sign of the Three Candles, 1957.
McGahern, John. *The Barracks*. London: Faber and Faber Lim-
     ited, 1963.
_____. *The Dark*. London: Faber and Faber, 1965.
Meenan, James and David Webb (eds.). *A View of Ireland*.
     Dublin: Hely's Limited, 1957.
Mercier, Vivian. *The Irish Comic Tradition*. Oxford: At the Clar-
     endon Press, 1962.
Merriman, Bryan. *The Midnight Court* (tr. by David Marcus).
     Dublin: The Dolmen Press, 1967.
Messenger, Betty T. *The Folklore of the Northern Irish Linen
     Industry*. Ann Arbor: Michigan University Microfilms, 1975.
Messenger, John C. "Anthropologist at Play: The Research Im-
     plications of Balladmongering." *American Anthropologist*,
     66 (1964), 407-16.
_____. "A Critical Reexamination of the Concept of Spirits: With
     Special Reference to Traditional Irish Folklore and Contem-
     porary Irish Folk Culture." *American Anthropologist*, 64
     (1962),367-73.
_____. Film review of *The Village. American Anthropologist*, 74
     (1972), 1577-81.
_____. "Folk Religion." In *Folklore and Folklife*, ed. Richard N.
     Dorson. Chicago: University of Chicago Press, 1972, pp.
     217-32.
_____. *Inis Beag: Isle of Ireland*. New York: Holt, Rinehart and
     Winston, Inc., 1969.
_____. "Islands of Saints, Scholars, and Scléip." *Natural History*,
     83 (1974), 62-9 and 114.

———. "Joe O'Donnell, Seanchai of Aran." *Journal of the Folklore Institute*, 1 (1964), 197-213.

———. "Man of Aran Revisited: An Anthropological Critique." *Irish University Review*, 3 (1966), 15-47.

———. "Montserrat: 'The Most Distinctively Irish Settlement in the New World.'" *Ethnicity*, 2 (1975), 281-303.

———. "Sex and Repression in an Irish Folk Community." In *Human Sexual Behavior*, eds. Donald S. Marshall and Robert C. Suggs. New York: Basic Books, Inc., 1971, pp. 3-37.

Michaelson, Evalyn K. and Walter Goldschmidt. "Female Roles and Male Dominance Among Peasants." *Southwestern Journal of Anthropology*, 27 (1971), 330-52.

Mogey, J. M. *Rural Life in Northern Ireland*. London: Oxford University Press, 1947.

Mould, Daphne D. C. Pochin. *The Aran Islands*. Newton Abbot: David & Charles, 1972.

Mullen, Pat. *Hero Breed*. London: Faber and Faber Limited, 1936.

———. *Man of Aran*. London: Faber and Faber Limited, 1934.

Murphy, H. B. M. "Alcoholism and Schizophrenia in the Irish: A Review." *Transcultural Psychiatric Research Review*, 12 (1975).

Murphy, Michael J. *At Slieve Gullion's Foot*. Dundalk: W. Tempest Ltd., 1945.

———. *Mountain Year*. Chester Springs. Penn.: Dufour Editions, Inc., 1965.

———. *Now You're Talking . . . Folk Tales from the North of Ireland*. Belfast: Blackstaff Press, 1976.

———. *Tyrone Folk Quest*. Belfast: Blackstaff Press, 1973.

Murphy, Robert C. "The Timeless Arans." *National Geographic*, 59 (1931), 747-75.

Murray, William C. *Michael Joe*. New York: Popular Library, 1965.

Nemec, Thomas F. "The Irish Emigration to Newfoundland." *The Newfoundland Quarterly*, 4 (1972), 15-24.

Newman, Jeremiah (ed.). *The Limerick Rural Survey*. Tipperary: Muintir na Tire Rural Publications, 1964.

O'Brien, Conor Cruise. *States of Ireland*. New York: Pantheon Books, 1972.

O'Brien, Edna. *The Country Girls.* London: Hutchinson, 1960.

O'Brien, John A. (ed.). *The Vanishing Irish.* London: W. H. Allen, 1954.

O'Brien, Liam. *The Magic Wisp: A History of the Mentally Ill in Ireland.* Unpublished manuscript, n.d.

O'Brien, T. *History of the Aran Islands.* Unpublished manuscript, 1945.

O´ Crohan, Tomás. *The Islandman.* Oxford: At the Clarendon Press, 1951.

O´ Cuív, Brian (ed.). *A View of the Irish Language.* Dublin: Stationery Office, 1969.

O'Faolain, Seán. *The Irish.* Harmondsworth: Penguin Books, 1969.

O'Flaherty, Liam. *Famine.* London: Victor Gollancz, Ltd., 1937.

––––––. *Skerrett.* London: Gollancz, 1932.

––––––. *Thy Neighbour's Wife.* London: Jonathan Cape, 1923.

O Flaherty, Tom. *Aranmen All.* Dublin: At the Sign of the Three Candles, 1936.

––––––. *Cliffmen of the West.* Dublin: At the Sign of the Three Candles, 1936.

O'Hanlon, Thomas J. *The Irish.* New York: Harper & Row, Publishers, 1975.

O'Neill, Conor. "The Social Function of Physical Violence in an Irish Urban Area." *The Economic and Social Review,* 2 (1971), 11-22.

O'Neill-Barna, Anne. *Himself and I.* New York: The Citadel Press, 1957.

Opler, Marvin K. *Culture and Social Psychiatry.* New York: Atherton Press, 1967, 163-4 and 287-303.

O´ Súilleabháin, Seán. *A Handbook of Irish Folklore.* Hatboro: Folkore Associates, Inc., 1963.

––––––. *Irish Folk Custom and Belief.* Dublin: At the Three Candles, Ltd., 1967.

––––––. *Irish Wake Amusements.* Cork: The Mercier Press, 1967.

O'Sullivan, Maurice. *Twenty Years A-Growing.* London: Oxford University Press, 1968.

O'Sullivan, Sean. *Folktales of Ireland.* Chicago: University of Chicago Press, 1966.

O´ Tauthaigh, Gearóid. *Ireland Before the Famine, 1798-1848.* Dublin: Gill and Macmillan, 1972.

Phádraig, Máire Nic Ghiolla. "Bibliography of the Social Aspects of the Legal System, Politics, Administration in Ireland." *Social Studies*, 1 (1972), 480-98.

_____. "Bibliography of the Social Sciences in Ireland." *Social Studies*, 2 (1973), 75-90.

_____. "Bibliography of the Sociology of Education in Ireland." *Social Studies*, 1 (1972), 350-66.

_____. "Bibliography of the Sociology of Religion in Ireland." *Social Studies*, 1 (1972), 246-62.

_____. "Select Bibliography of Social Problems and Services." *Social Studies*, 1 (1972), 94-111.

Potter,George W. *To the Golden Door*. Boston: Little, Brown and Company, 1960.

Power, Richard. *The Land of Youth*. New York: The Dial Press, 1964.

Pritchett, V. S. and Evelyn Hofer. *Dublin: A Portrait*. London: The Bodley Head, 1967.

Quinn, David B. *The Elizabethans and the Irish*. Ithaca: Cornell University Press, 1966.

Rivers, Elizabeth. *Stranger in Aran*. Dublin: The Cuala Press, 1946.

Roche, V. S. *Inishmore: A Microcosm of Ireland*. Thesis, Trinity College, Dublin, 1971.

Rohan, Dorine. *Marriage Irish Style*. Cork: The Mercier Press, 1969.

St. Clair, Sheila. *Folklore of the Ulster People*. Cork: The Mercier Press, 1971.

Salaman, R. N. *The History and Social Influence of the Potato*. London: Cambridge University Press, 1949.

Sayers, Peig. *An Old Woman's Reflections*. London: Oxford University Press, 1962.

Schrier, Arnold. *Ireland and the American Emigration 1850-1900*. Minneapolis: University of Minnesota Press, 1958.

Shannon, William V. *The American Irish*. New York: The Macmillan Company, 1963.

Sheehy, Michael. *Divided We Stand: A Study of Partition*. London: Faber and Faber, 1955.

_____. *Is Ireland Dying?* London: Hollis & Carter, 1968.

Skelton, Robin. *The Writings of J. M. Synge*. London: Thames and Hudson, 1971.

*Social Studies.* "Research in Progress in Ireland." 2 (1973), 179-93.

Stephens, Nicholas and Robin E. Glasscock (eds.). *Irish Geographical Studies in Honour of E. Estyn Evans.* Belfast: The Queen's University, Department of Geography, 1970.

Streib, Gordon F. "Attitudes of the Irish Toward Changes in the Catholic Church." *Social Compass,* 20 (1973), 49-71.

_____. "Farmers and Urbanites: Attitudes Toward Intergenerational Relations in Ireland." *Rural Sociology,* 35 (1970), 26-39.

_____. "Migration and Filial Bonds: Attitudes of Cork Farmers and Dublin Men." *Irish Journal of Agricultural Economics and Rural Sociology,* 3 (1970), 61-73.

_____. "Old Age in Ireland: Demographic and Sociological Aspects." *The Gerontologist,* 8 (1968), 227-35.

_____. "The Restoration of the Irish Language: Behavioral and Symbolic Aspects." *Ethnicity,* 1 (1974), 73-89.

_____. "Social Stratification in the Republic of Ireland: The Horizontal and the Vertical Mosaic." *Ethnology,* 12 (1973), 341-57.

Swain, J. "Achill Island: A Regional Survey." *Brycgstowe,* 1 (1970), 37-47.

Swinfen, Averil. *The Irish Donkey.* Cork: The Mercier Press, 1969.

Synge, John M. *The Aran Islands.* Dublin: Maunsel & Co., Ltd., 1907.

_____. *The Complete Plays of John M. Synge.* New York: Vintage Books, 1960.

_____. "A Dream of Inishmaan." *The Gael,* March 1904, p. 93.

_____. "The Last Fortress of the Celt." *The Gael,* April 1901, pp. 109-13.

Thomas, Veronica and Winfield Parks. "The Arans, Ireland's Invincible Isles." *National Geographic,* 139 (1971), 545-73.

Tracy, Honor. *The Quiet End of Evening.* New York: Random House, 1972.

_____. *The Straight and Narrow Path.* New York: Random House, 1956.

Tracy, Robert (ed). *The Aran Islands and Other Writings of John M. Synge.* New York: Vintage Books, 1962.

Ussher, Arland. *The Face and Mind of Ireland.* London: Victor Gollancz, 1949.

Viney, Michael. *The Broken Marriage*. Dublin: The Irish Times, 1970.

Vyvyan, C. C. "The Aran Islands." *The Cornhill Magazine*, 156 (1937), pp. 328-40.

Walsh, Brendan. "Some Irish Population Problems Reconsidered." *The Economic and Social Research Institute Paper No. 42*, 1968.

Walsh, Jane. *The Social Organisation of an Island Community in Western Ireland: Clare Island, County Mayo*. Diss., University of Edinburgh, 1958.

Westropp, Thomas J. "A Folklore Survey of County Clare." *Folk-Lore*, 21-3 (1910-12).

_____. "A Study of Folklore on the Coast of Connacht." *Folk-Lore*, 29-32 (1918-20).

Whyte, John H. *Church and State in Modern Ireland*. Dublin: Gill & Macmillan, 1971.

Wilson, Sloan. "Ireland and the Irish." *Fact*, 3 (1966), 28-37.

Wittke, Carl. *The Irish in America*. Baton Rouge: Louisiana State University Press, 1956.

Woodham-Smith, Cecil. *The Great Hunger*. London: Hamish Hamilton, 1962.

# Index